Copyright

Introduction

Did you know that people watch 5 billion videos on YouTube every day? In fact, 300 hundred hours of video are uploaded to YouTube every minute!

This might not even surprise you, as YouTube is the leading service that made it possible to easily put videos online in 2005. Flash forward to 2017 and if your marketing strategy does not have a video component tied to it, your visibility and business growth potential will suffer. Video should become a critical piece of the marketing puzzle because of how much video content your audience is consuming.

But, with many other companies knowing this, it's becoming harder and harder to stand out amongst your competition. This is why advertising spend does need to be allocated to services like YouTube in order to gain visibility from your target audience.

Although similar to paid search spend, the world of YouTube advertising can seem a bit overwhelming and complicated to navigate at first.

Hence, this guide will walk you through the several aspects of running a successful YouTube channel and make a killing using these tips.

Chapter 1
About YouTube

YouTube is the leader in online video, and the premier destination to watch, share, and promote original videos online. YouTube is fully integrated with Google Ad Words for video, leveling the playing field for businesses that want to reach new customers with online video.

YouTube is a video Social Networking site and the 2nd most popular search site on the Internet after Google, who owns YouTube. YouTube video watching is a significant activity on the Internet, with over 1 billion visits to YourTube daily and over 100 million videos watched daily. And it's easy for anyone who sees your video to rate it and share it with his Social Network.

How YouTube Works?

YouTube's theme is "Broadcast Yourself," and as such encourages everyone to make and broadcast videos on everything imaginable. YouTube is owned and operated by Google, and leverages the search power of Google.

All YouTube videos are indexed by Google's search and will appear in Google's search results when you select Video in the search options on Google. Using YouTube is a great way to get listed in Google's search results since Google gives YouTube videos priority in their search results.

YouTube videos can be viewed by anyone with access to the Web site. No user account or log-in is needed to search for or watch videos. Setting up a user account, on the other hand, allows you to upload videos, and also lets you customize your viewing with YouTube by subscribing to "channels" and giving feedback ratings on videos.

When you set up your own YouTube user account, many of the familiar functions of Social Networking are offered as options, such as sending a YouTube video link to a friend or contact, commenting on a video, and rating a video. You can also link to a YouTube video from your blog and include it in a post.

Using YouTube for Marketing

Videos on YouTube can be short and simple. For your marketing, decide on a goal for your YouTube activity. Some common themes include customer support, educational, product instructions, customer interviews, employee interviews, event videos, and professional produced videos.

Your YouTube videos need to have tags and descriptions associated with them for search in YouTube, so use your keywords and be sure to include them when you upload your video. Google's search bots cannot index the media, only the text associated with the media, so adding tags is critical to your video being indexed.

Just like any Social Media, creating an account and only posting once (one Video) won't have a great impact. Creating a series of videos, however, will result in increased search optimization and followers of your YouTube channel. Find a way to implement regular video production into your marketing effort to build an audience on YouTube and increase your ranking.

Video Production

For production, you can use a hand-held video camera. Any major brand that has a microphone input will produce good video. Good sound quality is important for video production and making your YouTube video easy to understand. If you have a story to tell, make some notes and rehearse those several times to make it sound more natural when you are reading from them.

If you find you're better at ad-hoc video, keep a video camera with you for part to capture some of your daily activities. If you have a Smartphone, use the built-in video camera to capture some short videos. Simple YouTube uploading from a YouTube app is usually a feature included with most smart phones.

Microsoft Windows Live Movie Maker and the Apple iMovie applications allow basic video editing and are a good place to start for editing your own video productions. Consider getting a professional video made if you decide to expand your marketing and want more complex stories told in your videos. The production quality on YouTube is improving and a good video production can be created for $1,000-$4,000 as a starting point. The higher the budget, the more you'll get in scripting, production preparation, and concept development by a professional. But don't let that stop you from doing something on your own, good audio quality and a steady camera can result in an excellent video.

Remember, it's the message and content that's important to viewers.

YouTube Analytics

YouTube Analytics is a self-service analytics and reporting tool. It provides data about each video you upload, so you can easily track how many views it gets, where people are coming from to find it and what type of people are watching it.

YouTube Analytics can give you information about:

- the 'firsts' for the video, including the first referral from a related video, first referral from a YouTube search (including the search terms used), first time the video is embedded in another website
- how many views came from each referral source
- which gender and age groups the video is most popular with
- which countries the video is most popular in
- how many comments and ratings it has received.

YouTube channels

You can set up a YouTube channel for your business, bringing all your videos together. This allows you to customize your channel with images representing your firm. Your channel includes an 'About' section where you can provide a short description of your business and a link to your website or contact details.

Your channel is where you group the videos you make and upload, the videos you watch and like, and the playlists of videos you create.

Your channel will have a web address (URL) that you can promote on your website or marketing material. People can subscribe to your channel. This means when they log in to YouTube your videos will be listed on their YouTube homepage.

You can also create 'playlists' within your YouTube channel to organize your videos by subject or type. For example, you could have a playlist featuring videos about each of your product categories, or you might have a playlist for videos contributed by your customers for a video competition you run.

YouTube Advertising

YouTube incorporates features that let businesses promote their videos to people who might be interested in them, targeting customers by demographics, topics or interests.

Advertisers pay each time someone views their video. You can choose which locations your ad will appear in, what format it will be, and even how much you are prepared to pay per view (if you want to boost the prominence of your ad over your competitors). YouTube's advertising guide explains how it works.

Why Opt for YouTube for Business?

Starting a business and making sure that it prospers into something profitable – these are two completely different tasks. You need to put in a lot of effort to make sure that people see your product or brand. YouTube is one of the best possible tools for this job. Here are some of the important benefits that your business will get by building a strong presence on YouTube.

- **Popularize your product:** If your business is trying to get into a new market with a particular product, you can simply make a video of the product working and show the benefits that the product has. If done in a creative manner, you will soon find that there will be many people liking your video and going for your product.

- **Get feedback:** You can use YouTube even if you are not completely ready with your product. It can be a great tool to figure out the response that the product might get. You simply have to put up the video of your prototype.

- **Sharing made easy:** As a young business setup, you may have people located at remote locations. It might not be possible for you to share all the material with them. YouTube can be a great way to share presentations or something similar with these remote employees.

- **Simplify tasks:** For businesses that often get client calls regarding problems with the product, YouTube can be a lifesaver. You might not have a work force to cater to all these problems. In that case, you can simply make a video with systematic details and share it on YouTube so the users can access it.

- **Increase your brand visibility:** If you are unable to make a video regarding your business due to time constraints or lack of good content, then there are other methods. You can simply go, rate and comment on relevant

- videos. You can also share some good videos on your channel. Simply by doing this, you are making your brand more visible and communicating with other users.

- **YouTube Insight:** Once you have your video on YouTube, comments are not the only way to analyze them. In addition to comments and ratings, there is an Insight feature also available on YouTube. This is a reporting function, which provides you with statistical data regarding the people visiting your video. This is helpful as you can figure out whether your campaign is actually working or not and make changes accordingly.

- **Increase your site's traffic:** YouTube also allows you to insert links into your videos. By doing this you can channel traffic from your YouTube video to your own site. Search engines also index these videos, and video results are comparatively lesser than text results. This increases the chances of a person finding your business video through a search.

- **Save Money:** One of the most important factors in any marketing campaign is money. Conventional methods like advertising on television or newspaper require a lot of money, but YouTube allows you to upload your videos completely free. From setting up your channel to analyzing the traffic on your video, it costs you nothing.

- **YouTube Ads:** With such a huge number of views everyday YouTube is one site where you would definitely want to run an ad campaign. You have multiple options available when it comes to the kind of advertising campaign you want to run. You can use one of the several marketing programs or you can use the video target tool to place your ads.

Get the Maximum Out of YouTube

You can build your company's presence on YouTube, but the job is only half done. To make sure that your campaign succeeds, you have to put in a lot of effort. The most important thing would be make proper use of your channel. YouTube gives you the option of customizing how your channel looks. You should take full advantage of this as it allows you to stand out amongst other regular channels, and makes a positive impact on the viewer.

Many companies simply ignore their channel. After the initial bursts of enthusiasm, you may find that there is nothing happening in the channel and this may discourage you. Even if you have nothing new to post, make sure that you keep up to date with the comments.

You should also make sure that you keep your content organized. You have the option of creating playlists. So you can group all the relevant videos together into a single playlist, or you can sort them on the basis of time.

YouTube is one of the fastest growing sites and is a great platform for you to showcase your company. When it comes to social media marketing there are very few sites more important than YouTube. All you need to do is make full use of the features provided by the site and be patient. YouTube can do wonders for your business if used correctly.

Chapter 2
The Technical Guide to setting up a YouTube Channel – Step by Step

1. Channel features for YouTube creators

Use YouTube's channel features to customize your channel and support your brand. These features are available to all creators who have verified accounts.

To see what features you're currently eligible for, go to your account features page.

- **Monetization:** If you meet the monetization criteria, you can enable monetization to earn money from ads on videos.
- **Longer videos:** When your account is verified, you can upload videos longer than the 15-minute limit.
- **Link to external sites:** Use annotations in videos to link to external sites.
- **Custom thumbnails:** Upload a custom thumbnail for your video.

- **Content ID appeals:** Appeal rejected Content ID disputes.
- **Unlisted and private videos:** Make your videos unlisted and share your private videos.
- **Live events:** Learn how to create a live streaming event.
- **Series playlists:** Group videos into series playlists to help viewers discover them.
- **Customize channel layout:** Customize your channel's layout with branded banners and channel trailers.
- **Hangouts on Air:** You can create a live Hangout on Air event.
- **Video editor:** Edit your videos' content using the YouTube Video Editor.

2. Manage your channel with Creator Studio

You can use Creator Studio in YouTube to organize your channel, manage videos, and interact with fans. You can go directly to Creator Studio or follow these steps to navigate to your Creator Studio:

1. Sign in to your channel at www.youtube.com.
2. In the top right, click your account icon.
3. Click **Creator Studio**.

Tools in Creator Studio

- **Dashboard:** Check for notifications and alerts from YouTube, including the latest updates, stats, and notifications for your review.
- **Video Manager:** Organize and update your videos from one place or dig into a particular video to adjust settings individually. Use tools to optimize a video, tweak its settings, or bulk update changes across videos with a single click.
- **Community:** Communicate and collaborate with your fans and fellow creators. Review and respond to comments, read private messages, see videos where you've been credited, or review a list of fans (if your channel has at least 1,000 subscribers).
- **Channel:** Adjust settings that affect your channel overall, such as signing up for monetization, controlling your upload defaults, or enabling live streaming.
- **Analytics:** Review your channel's performance and get info on how your channel is growing. Find reports and data to help you evaluate your channel and video performance, including views, subscribers, watch time, revenue for partners, and more.

- **Create:** Access the audio library and video editor to create new videos, add sound effects or unique music, or experiment with transitions.

3. Basics about your channel

Your channel is where you can organize your video content for your audience. As a channel owner, you can add videos, playlists, and information about yourself or your channel for visitors to explore.

Classic desktop experience

1. Sign in to your YouTube account on a computer.
2. On the left, select **My channel**.
3. Use the drop-down menu next to your name to view your channel as **Yourself**, a **New visitor**, or a **Returning subscriber**. When you want to go back to viewing as yourself, click **Done** at the top of the screen.
4. Use the tabs to navigate previewing the channel:

- **Home:** This is what your audience sees when they visit your channel. They can view a feed of your activities or preview different sections of your customized layout.

- **Videos:** Use this to see a list of all uploads publicly available for subscribers or all of the videos you've publicly liked. You can sort by most popular or date added.
- **Playlists:** This is a list of all the playlists that you've created.
- **Discussion:** If you've turned on the discussion tab, this will display comments left on your channel.
- **About:** Use this to add a channel description (maximum length of 1,000 characters), set your channel country, enter a business contact email address, and define social or other web links.
- Links that you add here are featured just below your description and use the icon from the corresponding social network when displayed. You can overlay up to five of these links on your channel art as shortcut icons.
- To edit your About tab, hover over the content, then click edit.

New desktop experience

1. Sign in to your YouTube account on a computer.
2. Under your profile picture at the top right, select **My channel**.
3. Click **Edit Layout.**

1. Use the drop-down menu next to your name to view your channel as **Yourself**, a **New visitor**, or a **Returning subscriber**. When you want to go back to viewing as yourself, click **Done** at the top of the screen.
2. Use the tabs to navigate previewing the channel:

*   **Home:** This is what your audience sees when they visit your channel. They can view a feed of your activities or preview different sections of your customized layout.
*   **Videos:** Use this to see a list of all uploads publicly available for subscribers or all of the videos you've publicly liked. You can sort by most popular or date added.
*   **Playlists:** This is a list of all the playlists that you've created.
*   **Discussion:** If you've turned on the discussion tab, this will display comments left on your channel.
*   **About:** Use this to add a channel description (maximum length of 1,000 characters), set your channel country, enter a business contact email address, and define social or other web links.
*   Links that you add here are featured just below your description and use the icon

- from the corresponding social network when displayed. You can overlay up to five of these links on your channel art as shortcut icons.
- To edit your about tab, hover over the content, then click edit.

4. Turn comments on or off

Classic desktop experience

- **Manage channel settings**

You can decide if you want to allow viewers to comment on your channel.

1. Sign in to your YouTube account on a computer.
2. On the left, select **My channel**.
3. Under your channel banner, click settings.
4. Turn **Show discussion tab** on or off.
5. If you have the discussion tab turned on, chose a comments setting:

- **Display automatically:** Comments will always show on your channel.
- **Don't display until approved:** Comments won't show on your channel until you approve them.

Comments are not available on private videos. If you want to allow comments on a video that's not publicly available, post an unlisted video instead.

- **Manage video settings**

You can decide if you want to allow viewers to comment on specific videos.

1. Sign in to your YouTube account on a computer.
2. Go to Creator Studio > Video Manager.
3. Select the box next to any of the videos you want to manage.
4. At the top of the screen, click the **Actions** menu.
5. Select More actions > Comments.
6. Select or unselect **Do not allow comments**.

- **New desktop experience**

- **Manage channel settings**

You can decide if you want to allow viewers to comment on your channel.

1. Sign in to your YouTube account on a computer.

1. Under your avatar at the top right, select **My channel**.
2. Under your channel banner, click settings .
3. Turn **Show discussion tab** on or off.
4. If you have the discussion tab turned on, chose a comments setting:

- **Display automatically:** Comments will always show on your channel.
- **Don't display until approved:** Comments won't show on your channel until you approve them.

Comments are not available on private videos. If you want to allow comments on a video that's not publicly available, post an unlisted video instead.

- **Manage video settings**

You can decide if you want to allow viewers to comment on specific videos.

1. Sign in to your YouTube account on a computer.
2. Go to Creator Studio > Video Manager.
3. Select the box next to any of the videos you want to manage.
4. At the top of the screen, click the **Actions** menu.

1. Select More actions > Comments.
2. Select or unselect **Do not allow comments**.
3. An important step in managing and promoting a YouTube channel is to add the right channel keywords.

Keywords can indeed help users to discover your YouTube channel when they make searches on Google, YouTube and other search engines. So the first step is to choose the keywords that specifically represent your channel and the type of content published.

Once done, sign-in to YouTube, click on your profile picture displayed at the top right corner > **Creator Studio** > **Channel** > **Advanced**:

Type your keywords in the **Channel Keywords** field and then click on **Save**:

Separate your keywords with a space and use quotation marks when search terms are in the form of short phrases.

1. Create or edit channel art

Channel art shows as a banner at the top of your YouTube page. You can use it to brand your channel's identity and give your page a unique look and feel.

Use the guidelines and examples below to set up your design. Keep in mind that channel art looks different on desktop, mobile, and TV displays.

Add or change channel art

1. On a computer, sign in to your YouTube account.
2. In the top right menu, select **My Channel**.
   - **New channel art:** Near the top of the screen, click **Add channel art**.
   - **Existing channel art:** Hover your cursor over the existing banner until you see the **edit** icon. Click the icon and select **Edit channel art**.
3. Upload an image or photo from your computer or saved photos. You can also click the **Gallery** tab to choose an image from the YouTube photo library.
4. You'll see a preview of how the art will appear across different devices. To make changes, select **Adjust the crop**.
5. Click **Select**.

6. Verification badges on channels

When you see a or verification checkmark next to a YouTube channel's name, it means that the channel belongs to an established creator or is the official channel of a brand, business, or organization.

Verification badges don't affect search results for the channel or grant access to additional features on YouTube.

How to get a verification badge

Eligibility criteria

Once your channel gets 100,000 subscribers, you're eligible to submit a request to YouTube for a verification badge. Note that we've made changes to this process over time, so you may see many types of channels with verification badges on YouTube. **Note:** If you're an advertiser interested in a verification badge, contact your sales manager to learn more.

Keeping your verification badge

Once you have a verification badge, it'll stay on your channel even if your channel's subscriber number changes. If you change your channel's name, you can't keep the verification badge for the renamed channel.

YouTube reserves the right to revoke your verification badge or terminate your channel if you violate our Community Guidelines or the YouTube Terms of Service.

Manage your channel icon

Your channel icon shows over your channel art banner. It's the icon that displays to other users for your videos and channel on YouTube watch pages.

The default icon for your channel is the image associated with your Google Account. You can see this image in the top right corner of the page when you're logged into YouTube and other Google services. If you want to change this image, you can modify it in your Google Account settings.

7. Channel icon specs

Use these recommended guidelines when creating a new channel icon. Do not upload pictures containing celebrities, nudity, artwork, or copyrighted images since this violates our Community Guidelines.

- JPG, GIF, BMP, or PNG file (no animated GIFs)
- 800 X 800 px image (recommended)
- Square or round image that renders at 98 X 98 px

Edit & update channel icon

You can choose to upload a new image, use a still frame from one of your uploaded videos, or use your default image.

Classic desktop experience

1. Sign in to your YouTube account.
2. On the left, select **My Channel**.
3. Hover over your existing channel icon in the top left of your channel art banner.
4. Click the edit icon .
5. Click **Edit** and follow the on-screen instructions to select the new image.

New desktop experience

1. Sign in to your YouTube account.
2. Under your profile photo at the top right, select **My Channel**.
3. Hover over your existing channel icon in the top left of your channel art banner.
4. Click the edit icon .
5. Click **Edit** and follow the on-screen instructions to select the new image.

8. Customize channel layout

You can customize the layout of your channel so that viewers see what you want them to when they get to your page. If you don't customize the layout, all visitors will see your channel feed.

This is recommended for creators who upload videos regularly. You can add a channel trailer, suggest content for your subscribers, and organize all your videos and playlists into sections. Or, for example, you can always show your channel trailer to new visitors.

Before you can customize your layout, you need to turn this feature on:

1. On a computer, sign in to your YouTube account.
2. In the left menu, click **My Channel**.
3. Under your channel's banner, click the settings icon.
4. Toggle **Customize the layout of your channel** to on.
5. Click **Save**.

After you've enabled channel customization, follow the instructions to create a channel trailer for new visitors and create channel sections to customize the layout on your channel.

9. Organize content with channel sections

You can organize and promote content that you want to highlight on your channel using channel sections. A section lets you group videos together in a particular way so that your audience can make easier decisions about what they want to watch. You can have up to 10 sections on one channel.

10. Create a channel trailer for new viewers

You can have a video trailer show to all unsubscribed visitors to your channel. Your channel trailer is like a movie trailer - use it as a way to offer a preview of your channel's offerings so viewers will want to subscribe. You can't currently watch channel trailers on the YouTube mobile apps.

By default, ads won't appear when the trailer is playing on the channel page in the trailer spot (unless the video you've chosen contains third-party claimed content). This helps keep the user focused on learning about and subscribing to your channel. If the viewer is already subscribed to your channel, they'll see a video under "What to Watch Next" instead.

11. Set a channel trailer

Before you start: To set up a channel trailer, you have to first turn on channel customization for the channel.

1. Upload the video you want to be your channel trailer.
2. Go to the channel you want to manage.
3. Click the **For new visitors** tab. If you don't see the "For new visitors" tab, follow these instructions to turn on channel customization for the channel.
4. Click on **Channel trailer**.
5. Choose the video by selecting its thumbnail or entering its URL.

Note: If the visitor to your channel is already subscribed to your channel, they won't see your trailer. Instead, they'll see a video under "What to Watch Next." Follow these instructions to set the featured content you want to show.

Quick tips for creating channel trailers

- Assume the viewer has never heard of you.
- Keep it short.
- Hook your viewers in the first few seconds.
- Show, don't tell.
- Ask viewers to subscribe in your video and with annotations.

Find out more about how to produce a captivating channel trailer that hooks your viewers and turns them into subscribers.

Change or remove the channel trailer

1. Go to the channel you want to manage.
2. Hover over your channel name and click the edit icon.
3. Select **Change trailer** or **Remove trailer**.

12. Global Audience: Best practices for localized channels

As your audience continues to grow and your channel reaches global communities speaking varied languages, it's common to consider whether it makes sense to separate content by language into individual, localized channels, or continue to maintain one larger (global) channel with multiple language content. Brands and advertisers often turn to one of three models to address their global audiences but ultimately it's up to you to decide what works best for your channel and audience.

A. **One channel with multiple language content**

In this model, brands establish one main channel where content is uploaded in multiple languages for multiple geographies.

In this model, brands establish one main channel where content is uploaded in multiple languages for multiple geographies.

Branding

With one channel to represent your brand presence, your brand and any associated assets will be consistent across regions. If your audience uses the same terms for search across languages (ex. a product name) this channel will be highly relevant and easy to discover.

Engagement

Driving your audience to one global channel will consolidate your viewership and channel subscribers and make it easier for users to find your channel in YouTube search. Once discovered, it may prove more challenging to engage with your subscribers from across the world as a single audience since content can be available in varied languages. As such, your channel's audience will be fragmented by language, and your channel community will see posts, comments, and feed updates in many different languages. To help your audience stay engaged, you might consider adding subtitles and captions to your videos to make your content more accessible and available to a larger audience. You might also create unique sections and playlists on your channel for each key market to provide a consolidated offering by language and drive watch time.

Management

With all of your content in one place, your team can focus all resources on managing this single channel and make it easier to maintain consistent global branding and tone. Of course, the actual number of resources needed to manage a channel will depend entirely on the regularity of uploads planned and the intensity of your individual channel strategy. Being consistent with uploads, ensuring brand equity and audience management is critical to growing a successful channel.

B. Multiple channels each with unique language content

Here brands create multiple channels, each featuring different language and geography content. This can be very helpful for languages with various alphabets or search terms.

Branding

With a unique channel for each geography or language, brands will have the opportunity to customize each channel to the local audience and easily incorporate local events and promotions. If your brand identity varies slightly in different regions, this will allow you to respect those differences and incorporate them into your channel strategy.

Engagement

While your viewership and subscribers will be split across multiple channels by language preference, this does allow for you to have focused communications with a specific, engaged audience. All items on the channel will be targeted to a language specific audience which may result in an improved user experience. Users may be less likely to get confused or disengaged because of varying language content once they discover the brand channel in their preferred language. Don't forget that you'll want to specify which language a particular channel targets since users may see various channels available in search and typically larger channels trump smaller channels. It will be important to cross-promote your various language channels amongst each other to help improve discoverability. A great way to ensure that you're cross-promoting effectively is to add channels of interest to the "featured channels" section your channel's about tab.

Management

With your channel content spread across multiple regions/languages, each local channel will need to allocate resources to manage the channel on an ongoing basis. Whether your channels follow a predefined framework or rely on local teams to manage, you'll want to be sure your brand can devote enough resources to launch and maintain each channel with a regular upload and engagement schedule.

C. One global channel and supporting local channels

With a single channel to serve as the main brand hub to feature global campaigns in the main brand language and territory and supporting local channels targeting different languages and regions, brands can foster a larger global presence while still connecting to their local regions with specific content.

Branding

With this distribution of channel content, you can still showcase consistent global branding in your hub channel while using the various local channels to feature local events and promotions. It may be helpful to adopt templates for your video metadata and video thumbnails to help maintain brand consistency across your various channels.

Engagement

With so many channels, viewership and subscribers will be segmented across multiple channels but users are able to find the relevant content for their specific language and receive a consistent experience when viewing content and engaging with the channel community. It will be important to use the main global channel to help drive viewers to your local channels using video metadata, channel descriptions, and featured channel programming. Depending on upload frequency, more frequent uploads on the local channels may result in those channels receiving a more prominent placement in search.

Management

This channel organization structure requires coordination between global and local teams but allows for flexibility when it comes to customizing the brand message for local markets or featuring local campaigns. This may be the most resource-intensive channel organization structure as you will need to dedicate time to both a larger global channel and several local channels but the actual number of resources will depend on the regularity of uploads and engagement strategies implemented on each channel.

13. Opt in to channel recommendations

You can opt in to have your YouTube channel listed on other channels that your potential viewers might be watching. This section is called "Related channels" and you can see it on the right side of channel pages while using YouTube on a computer.

Channel recommendations are created based on:

- What channels are watched by the same users
- Whether the videos are about similar topics
- Whether the channels are suitable for the same audience

You can't control what channels appear in the "Related channels" section on your own channel, but you can opt out to remove the section completely.

14. Turn your channel recommendation on or off

1. Sign in to your YouTube channel.
2. In the top right, click your account icon > **Creator Studio**.
3. In the left menu, select **Channel > Advanced**.
4. Under "Channel recommendations," opt in or out:

- To opt in: Select "Allow my channel to appear in other channels' recommendations." This allows your channel to appear in "Related channels" sections across YouTube.
- **To opt out:** Select "Do not allow my channel to appear in other channels' recommendations." This removes the entire "Related channels" section from your channel page.

15. YouTube - How to add weblinks to your channel

Web links may include:

- A link to your social profiles (Twitter, Facebook...)
- Your email address.
- A link to your website or blog.

- Here's how to get started:
- Sign-in to your YouTube channel.
- Click on the *Menu button > My Channel*.
- Go to the About tab and click on **+Links**.
- Enter your email address in the first field:
- To add a link to your blog or website, scroll to the **CUSTOM LINKS** section and click on the *Add* button:
- To add a link to a social profile, scroll to the SOCIAL LINKS section and click on the Add button. Use the drop menu to select the service of your choice and paste the URL of your social profile in the adjacent field:

16. How to close a YouTube channel?

- First log-in to your YouTube account.
- Click on the small avatar located top-right > Settings
- In the Overview section, just under your Username, click on the Advanced button
- Click on the "Delete channel" button and follow the procedure.

17. Connecting a YouTube channel to your social accounts

This allows YouTube to share you public activity (new video upload, likes..) on your social channels.

The procedure is as follows:

- Sign-in to your YouTube channel.
- Go to YouTube Settings > Account Settings > Connected accounts:

To connect to a Facebook page or profile:

- Click on the Connect button.
- Enter your Facebook credentials and click on Log in:

Chapter 3
Tips on Starting a New and Successful YouTube Channel

Truth be told, there is no set formula for a successful YouTube channel. But there are a few key ingredients that will make your chances of YouTube fame all the more likely.

YouTube megastars like Ryan Higa, Ray William Johnson, and Bethany Mota have amassed billions of views simply through vlogging. This has almost certainly raked in seven figures or more in revenue, while leading to untold opportunities outside of YouTube.

And then there are the channels that house much *more* substance, while still remaining impressively popular. Take Creative Live, the Ask Gary Vee Show, and Big Think.

These channels may all be entirely different, but share the common factor of regularly being watched by huge numbers of people. This is because they've stuck to at least some of the key ingredients below.

- **Making the Most of Metadata**

Successful YouTube channels often need more than just engaging videos to become popular. The metadata — title, description, keywords, and tags — are incredibly important, too. It's based in large part on *this* data (in combination with other things) that YouTube ranks your videos in their search results. In other words, good metadata ensures your videos are discoverable.

Take Gary Vaynerchuk, for instance. His descriptions include timestamps that not only help viewers navigate his videos, but are also full of relevant keywords. Links mentioned in the video are posted in the description. There's also a short explanation about what different series' of Gary's videos are about, along with information on where you can find out more about him.

When it comes to crafting your own metadata, use resources such as YouTube's autocomplete search bar, YouTube Trends, and Google Trends to find the best keywords and tags to use. Include your most important link above the fold, as well as two sentences to describe the content within the video.

Also make sure to describe what your channel is about, and let people know where else they can follow you. Lastly, include a call to action

(usually asking people to subscribe to your channel).

If you're so inclined, producing and publishing a transcript of your YouTube video is also a sensible move.

- **Carefully Craft Your Title**

Your video titles should be short and snappy, offering a quick and intriguing insight into the content of your video. Don't forget to include your main keyword(s), too!

The best way to do this is to look at your title as if you'd never come across your brand before. Would you click on it? If you're not sure, change it. This often means moving any personal branding within the title to the end, so the main keywords appear first. It also means including episode numbers for serial content. And very importantly, be honest. Don't promise content that you don't deliver on.

- **Vary Your Content**

Speaking of content, in very broad terms, there are two kinds of content you can produce and publish on YouTube.

(usually asking people to subscribe to your channel).

If you're so inclined, producing and publishing a transcript of your YouTube video is also a sensible move.

- **Carefully Craft Your Title**

Your video titles should be short and snappy, offering a quick and intriguing insight into the content of your video. Don't forget to include your main keyword(s), too!

The best way to do this is to look at your title as if you'd never come across your brand before. Would you click on it? If you're not sure, change it. This often means moving any personal branding within the title to the end, so the main keywords appear first. It also means including episode numbers for serial content. And very importantly, be honest. Don't promise content that you don't deliver on.

- **Vary Your Content**

Speaking of content, in very broad terms, there are two kinds of content you can produce and publish on YouTube.

(usually asking people to subscribe to your channel).

If you're so inclined, producing and publishing a transcript of your YouTube video is also a sensible move.

- **Carefully Craft Your Title**

Your video titles should be short and snappy, offering a quick and intriguing insight into the content of your video. Don't forget to include your main keyword(s), too!

The best way to do this is to look at your title as if you'd never come across your brand before. Would you click on it? If you're not sure, change it. This often means moving any personal branding within the title to the end, so the main keywords appear first. It also means including episode numbers for serial content. And very importantly, be honest. Don't promise content that you don't deliver on.

- **Vary Your Content**

Speaking of content, in very broad terms, there are two kinds of content you can produce and publish on YouTube.

(usually asking people to subscribe to your channel).

If you're so inclined, producing and publishing a transcript of your YouTube video is also a sensible move.

- **Carefully Craft Your Title**

Your video titles should be short and snappy, offering a quick and intriguing insight into the content of your video. Don't forget to include your main keyword(s), too!

The best way to do this is to look at your title as if you'd never come across your brand before. Would you click on it? If you're not sure, change it. This often means moving any personal branding within the title to the end, so the main keywords appear first. It also means including episode numbers for serial content. And very importantly, be honest. Don't promise content that you don't deliver on.

- **Vary Your Content**

Speaking of content, in very broad terms, there are two kinds of content you can produce and publish on YouTube.

(usually asking people to subscribe to your channel).

If you're so inclined, producing and publishing a transcript of your YouTube video is also a sensible move.

- **Carefully Craft Your Title**

Your video titles should be short and snappy, offering a quick and intriguing insight into the content of your video. Don't forget to include your main keyword(s), too!

The best way to do this is to look at your title as if you'd never come across your brand before. Would you click on it? If you're not sure, change it. This often means moving any personal branding within the title to the end, so the main keywords appear first. It also means including episode numbers for serial content. And very importantly, be honest. Don't promise content that you don't deliver on.

- **Vary Your Content**

Speaking of content, in very broad terms, there are two kinds of content you can produce and publish on YouTube.

(usually asking people to subscribe to your channel).

If you're so inclined, producing and publishing a transcript of your YouTube video is also a sensible move.

- **Carefully Craft Your Title**

Your video titles should be short and snappy, offering a quick and intriguing insight into the content of your video. Don't forget to include your main keyword(s), too!

The best way to do this is to look at your title as if you'd never come across your brand before. Would you click on it? If you're not sure, change it. This often means moving any personal branding within the title to the end, so the main keywords appear first. It also means including episode numbers for serial content. And very importantly, be honest. Don't promise content that you don't deliver on.

- **Vary Your Content**

Speaking of content, in very broad terms, there are two kinds of content you can produce and publish on YouTube.

(usually asking people to subscribe to your channel).

If you're so inclined, producing and publishing a transcript of your YouTube video is also a sensible move.

- **Carefully Craft Your Title**

Your video titles should be short and snappy, offering a quick and intriguing insight into the content of your video. Don't forget to include your main keyword(s), too!

The best way to do this is to look at your title as if you'd never come across your brand before. Would you click on it? If you're not sure, change it. This often means moving any personal branding within the title to the end, so the main keywords appear first. It also means including episode numbers for serial content. And very importantly, be honest. Don't promise content that you don't deliver on.

- **Vary Your Content**

Speaking of content, in very broad terms, there are two kinds of content you can produce and publish on YouTube.

(usually asking people to subscribe to your channel).

If you're so inclined, producing and publishing a transcript of your YouTube video is also a sensible move.

- **Carefully Craft Your Title**

Your video titles should be short and snappy, offering a quick and intriguing insight into the content of your video. Don't forget to include your main keyword(s), too!

The best way to do this is to look at your title as if you'd never come across your brand before. Would you click on it? If you're not sure, change it. This often means moving any personal branding within the title to the end, so the main keywords appear first. It also means including episode numbers for serial content. And very importantly, be honest. Don't promise content that you don't deliver on.

- **Vary Your Content**

Speaking of content, in very broad terms, there are two kinds of content you can produce and publish on YouTube.

(usually asking people to subscribe to your channel).

If you're so inclined, producing and publishing a transcript of your YouTube video is also a sensible move.

- **Carefully Craft Your Title**

Your video titles should be short and snappy, offering a quick and intriguing insight into the content of your video. Don't forget to include your main keyword(s), too!

The best way to do this is to look at your title as if you'd never come across your brand before. Would you click on it? If you're not sure, change it. This often means moving any personal branding within the title to the end, so the main keywords appear first. It also means including episode numbers for serial content. And very importantly, be honest. Don't promise content that you don't deliver on.

- **Vary Your Content**

Speaking of content, in very broad terms, there are two kinds of content you can produce and publish on YouTube.

(usually asking people to subscribe to your channel).

If you're so inclined, producing and publishing a transcript of your YouTube video is also a sensible move.

- **Carefully Craft Your Title**

Your video titles should be short and snappy, offering a quick and intriguing insight into the content of your video. Don't forget to include your main keyword(s), too!

The best way to do this is to look at your title as if you'd never come across your brand before. Would you click on it? If you're not sure, change it. This often means moving any personal branding within the title to the end, so the main keywords appear first. It also means including episode numbers for serial content. And very importantly, be honest. Don't promise content that you don't deliver on.

- **Vary Your Content**

Speaking of content, in very broad terms, there are two kinds of content you can produce and publish on YouTube.

(usually asking people to subscribe to your channel).

If you're so inclined, producing and publishing a transcript of your YouTube video is also a sensible move.

- **Carefully Craft Your Title**

Your video titles should be short and snappy, offering a quick and intriguing insight into the content of your video. Don't forget to include your main keyword(s), too!

The best way to do this is to look at your title as if you'd never come across your brand before. Would you click on it? If you're not sure, change it. This often means moving any personal branding within the title to the end, so the main keywords appear first. It also means including episode numbers for serial content. And very importantly, be honest. Don't promise content that you don't deliver on.

- **Vary Your Content**

Speaking of content, in very broad terms, there are two kinds of content you can produce and publish on YouTube.

(usually asking people to subscribe to your channel).

If you're so inclined, producing and publishing a transcript of your YouTube video is also a sensible move.

- **Carefully Craft Your Title**

Your video titles should be short and snappy, offering a quick and intriguing insight into the content of your video. Don't forget to include your main keyword(s), too!

The best way to do this is to look at your title as if you'd never come across your brand before. Would you click on it? If you're not sure, change it. This often means moving any personal branding within the title to the end, so the main keywords appear first. It also means including episode numbers for serial content. And very importantly, be honest. Don't promise content that you don't deliver on.

- **Vary Your Content**

Speaking of content, in very broad terms, there are two kinds of content you can produce and publish on YouTube.

(usually asking people to subscribe to your channel).

If you're so inclined, producing and publishing a transcript of your YouTube video is also a sensible move.

- **Carefully Craft Your Title**

Your video titles should be short and snappy, offering a quick and intriguing insight into the content of your video. Don't forget to include your main keyword(s), too!

The best way to do this is to look at your title as if you'd never come across your brand before. Would you click on it? If you're not sure, change it. This often means moving any personal branding within the title to the end, so the main keywords appear first. It also means including episode numbers for serial content. And very importantly, be honest. Don't promise content that you don't deliver on.

- **Vary Your Content**

Speaking of content, in very broad terms, there are two kinds of content you can produce and publish on YouTube.

(usually asking people to subscribe to your channel).

If you're so inclined, producing and publishing a transcript of your YouTube video is also a sensible move.

- **Carefully Craft Your Title**

Your video titles should be short and snappy, offering a quick and intriguing insight into the content of your video. Don't forget to include your main keyword(s), too!

The best way to do this is to look at your title as if you'd never come across your brand before. Would you click on it? If you're not sure, change it. This often means moving any personal branding within the title to the end, so the main keywords appear first. It also means including episode numbers for serial content. And very importantly, be honest. Don't promise content that you don't deliver on.

- **Vary Your Content**

Speaking of content, in very broad terms, there are two kinds of content you can produce and publish on YouTube.

(usually asking people to subscribe to your channel).

If you're so inclined, producing and publishing a transcript of your YouTube video is also a sensible move.

- **Carefully Craft Your Title**

Your video titles should be short and snappy, offering a quick and intriguing insight into the content of your video. Don't forget to include your main keyword(s), too!

The best way to do this is to look at your title as if you'd never come across your brand before. Would you click on it? If you're not sure, change it. This often means moving any personal branding within the title to the end, so the main keywords appear first. It also means including episode numbers for serial content. And very importantly, be honest. Don't promise content that you don't deliver on.

- **Vary Your Content**

Speaking of content, in very broad terms, there are two kinds of content you can produce and publish on YouTube.

(usually asking people to subscribe to your channel).

If you're so inclined, producing and publishing a transcript of your YouTube video is also a sensible move.

- **Carefully Craft Your Title**

Your video titles should be short and snappy, offering a quick and intriguing insight into the content of your video. Don't forget to include your main keyword(s), too!

The best way to do this is to look at your title as if you'd never come across your brand before. Would you click on it? If you're not sure, change it. This often means moving any personal branding within the title to the end, so the main keywords appear first. It also means including episode numbers for serial content. And very importantly, be honest. Don't promise content that you don't deliver on.

- **Vary Your Content**

Speaking of content, in very broad terms, there are two kinds of content you can produce and publish on YouTube.

(usually asking people to subscribe to your channel).

If you're so inclined, producing and publishing a transcript of your YouTube video is also a sensible move.

- **Carefully Craft Your Title**

Your video titles should be short and snappy, offering a quick and intriguing insight into the content of your video. Don't forget to include your main keyword(s), too!

The best way to do this is to look at your title as if you'd never come across your brand before. Would you click on it? If you're not sure, change it. This often means moving any personal branding within the title to the end, so the main keywords appear first. It also means including episode numbers for serial content. And very importantly, be honest. Don't promise content that you don't deliver on.

- **Vary Your Content**

Speaking of content, in very broad terms, there are two kinds of content you can produce and publish on YouTube.

(usually asking people to subscribe to your channel).

If you're so inclined, producing and publishing a transcript of your YouTube video is also a sensible move.

- **Carefully Craft Your Title**

Your video titles should be short and snappy, offering a quick and intriguing insight into the content of your video. Don't forget to include your main keyword(s), too!

The best way to do this is to look at your title as if you'd never come across your brand before. Would you click on it? If you're not sure, change it. This often means moving any personal branding within the title to the end, so the main keywords appear first. It also means including episode numbers for serial content. And very importantly, be honest. Don't promise content that you don't deliver on.

- **Vary Your Content**

Speaking of content, in very broad terms, there are two kinds of content you can produce and publish on YouTube.

(usually asking people to subscribe to your channel).

If you're so inclined, producing and publishing a transcript of your YouTube video is also a sensible move.

- **Carefully Craft Your Title**

Your video titles should be short and snappy, offering a quick and intriguing insight into the content of your video. Don't forget to include your main keyword(s), too!

The best way to do this is to look at your title as if you'd never come across your brand before. Would you click on it? If you're not sure, change it. This often means moving any personal branding within the title to the end, so the main keywords appear first. It also means including episode numbers for serial content. And very importantly, be honest. Don't promise content that you don't deliver on.

- **Vary Your Content**

Speaking of content, in very broad terms, there are two kinds of content you can produce and publish on YouTube.

(usually asking people to subscribe to your channel).

If you're so inclined, producing and publishing a transcript of your YouTube video is also a sensible move.

- **Carefully Craft Your Title**

Your video titles should be short and snappy, offering a quick and intriguing insight into the content of your video. Don't forget to include your main keyword(s), too!

The best way to do this is to look at your title as if you'd never come across your brand before. Would you click on it? If you're not sure, change it. This often means moving any personal branding within the title to the end, so the main keywords appear first. It also means including episode numbers for serial content. And very importantly, be honest. Don't promise content that you don't deliver on.

- **Vary Your Content**

Speaking of content, in very broad terms, there are two kinds of content you can produce and publish on YouTube.

(usually asking people to subscribe to your channel).

If you're so inclined, producing and publishing a transcript of your YouTube video is also a sensible move.

- **Carefully Craft Your Title**

Your video titles should be short and snappy, offering a quick and intriguing insight into the content of your video. Don't forget to include your main keyword(s), too!

The best way to do this is to look at your title as if you'd never come across your brand before. Would you click on it? If you're not sure, change it. This often means moving any personal branding within the title to the end, so the main keywords appear first. It also means including episode numbers for serial content. And very importantly, be honest. Don't promise content that you don't deliver on.

- **Vary Your Content**

Speaking of content, in very broad terms, there are two kinds of content you can produce and publish on YouTube.

(usually asking people to subscribe to your channel).

If you're so inclined, producing and publishing a transcript of your YouTube video is also a sensible move.

- **Carefully Craft Your Title**

Your video titles should be short and snappy, offering a quick and intriguing insight into the content of your video. Don't forget to include your main keyword(s), too!

The best way to do this is to look at your title as if you'd never come across your brand before. Would you click on it? If you're not sure, change it. This often means moving any personal branding within the title to the end, so the main keywords appear first. It also means including episode numbers for serial content. And very importantly, be honest. Don't promise content that you don't deliver on.

- **Vary Your Content**

Speaking of content, in very broad terms, there are two kinds of content you can produce and publish on YouTube.

(usually asking people to subscribe to your channel).

If you're so inclined, producing and publishing a transcript of your YouTube video is also a sensible move.

- **Carefully Craft Your Title**

Your video titles should be short and snappy, offering a quick and intriguing insight into the content of your video. Don't forget to include your main keyword(s), too!

The best way to do this is to look at your title as if you'd never come across your brand before. Would you click on it? If you're not sure, change it. This often means moving any personal branding within the title to the end, so the main keywords appear first. It also means including episode numbers for serial content. And very importantly, be honest. Don't promise content that you don't deliver on.

- **Vary Your Content**

Speaking of content, in very broad terms, there are two kinds of content you can produce and publish on YouTube.

(usually asking people to subscribe to your channel).

If you're so inclined, producing and publishing a transcript of your YouTube video is also a sensible move.

- **Carefully Craft Your Title**

Your video titles should be short and snappy, offering a quick and intriguing insight into the content of your video. Don't forget to include your main keyword(s), too!

The best way to do this is to look at your title as if you'd never come across your brand before. Would you click on it? If you're not sure, change it. This often means moving any personal branding within the title to the end, so the main keywords appear first. It also means including episode numbers for serial content. And very importantly, be honest. Don't promise content that you don't deliver on.

- **Vary Your Content**

Speaking of content, in very broad terms, there are two kinds of content you can produce and publish on YouTube.

(usually asking people to subscribe to your channel).

If you're so inclined, producing and publishing a transcript of your YouTube video is also a sensible move.

- **Carefully Craft Your Title**

Your video titles should be short and snappy, offering a quick and intriguing insight into the content of your video. Don't forget to include your main keyword(s), too!

The best way to do this is to look at your title as if you'd never come across your brand before. Would you click on it? If you're not sure, change it. This often means moving any personal branding within the title to the end, so the main keywords appear first. It also means including episode numbers for serial content. And very importantly, be honest. Don't promise content that you don't deliver on.

- **Vary Your Content**

Speaking of content, in very broad terms, there are two kinds of content you can produce and publish on YouTube.

(usually asking people to subscribe to your channel).

If you're so inclined, producing and publishing a transcript of your YouTube video is also a sensible move.

- **Carefully Craft Your Title**

Your video titles should be short and snappy, offering a quick and intriguing insight into the content of your video. Don't forget to include your main keyword(s), too!

The best way to do this is to look at your title as if you'd never come across your brand before. Would you click on it? If you're not sure, change it. This often means moving any personal branding within the title to the end, so the main keywords appear first. It also means including episode numbers for serial content. And very importantly, be honest. Don't promise content that you don't deliver on.

- **Vary Your Content**

Speaking of content, in very broad terms, there are two kinds of content you can produce and publish on YouTube.

(usually asking people to subscribe to your channel).

If you're so inclined, producing and publishing a transcript of your YouTube video is also a sensible move.

- **Carefully Craft Your Title**

Your video titles should be short and snappy, offering a quick and intriguing insight into the content of your video. Don't forget to include your main keyword(s), too!

The best way to do this is to look at your title as if you'd never come across your brand before. Would you click on it? If you're not sure, change it. This often means moving any personal branding within the title to the end, so the main keywords appear first. It also means including episode numbers for serial content. And very importantly, be honest. Don't promise content that you don't deliver on.

- **Vary Your Content**

Speaking of content, in very broad terms, there are two kinds of content you can produce and publish on YouTube.

(usually asking people to subscribe to your channel).

If you're so inclined, producing and publishing a transcript of your YouTube video is also a sensible move.

- **Carefully Craft Your Title**

Your video titles should be short and snappy, offering a quick and intriguing insight into the content of your video. Don't forget to include your main keyword(s), too!

The best way to do this is to look at your title as if you'd never come across your brand before. Would you click on it? If you're not sure, change it. This often means moving any personal branding within the title to the end, so the main keywords appear first. It also means including episode numbers for serial content. And very importantly, be honest. Don't promise content that you don't deliver on.

- **Vary Your Content**

Speaking of content, in very broad terms, there are two kinds of content you can produce and publish on YouTube.

(usually asking people to subscribe to your channel).

If you're so inclined, producing and publishing a transcript of your YouTube video is also a sensible move.

- **Carefully Craft Your Title**

Your video titles should be short and snappy, offering a quick and intriguing insight into the content of your video. Don't forget to include your main keyword(s), too!

The best way to do this is to look at your title as if you'd never come across your brand before. Would you click on it? If you're not sure, change it. This often means moving any personal branding within the title to the end, so the main keywords appear first. It also means including episode numbers for serial content. And very importantly, be honest. Don't promise content that you don't deliver on.

- **Vary Your Content**

Speaking of content, in very broad terms, there are two kinds of content you can produce and publish on YouTube.

(usually asking people to subscribe to your channel).

If you're so inclined, producing and publishing a transcript of your YouTube video is also a sensible move.

- **Carefully Craft Your Title**

Your video titles should be short and snappy, offering a quick and intriguing insight into the content of your video. Don't forget to include your main keyword(s), too!

The best way to do this is to look at your title as if you'd never come across your brand before. Would you click on it? If you're not sure, change it. This often means moving any personal branding within the title to the end, so the main keywords appear first. It also means including episode numbers for serial content. And very importantly, be honest. Don't promise content that you don't deliver on.

- **Vary Your Content**

Speaking of content, in very broad terms, there are two kinds of content you can produce and publish on YouTube.

(usually asking people to subscribe to your channel).

If you're so inclined, producing and publishing a transcript of your YouTube video is also a sensible move.

- **Carefully Craft Your Title**

Your video titles should be short and snappy, offering a quick and intriguing insight into the content of your video. Don't forget to include your main keyword(s), too!

The best way to do this is to look at your title as if you'd never come across your brand before. Would you click on it? If you're not sure, change it. This often means moving any personal branding within the title to the end, so the main keywords appear first. It also means including episode numbers for serial content. And very importantly, be honest. Don't promise content that you don't deliver on.

- **Vary Your Content**

Speaking of content, in very broad terms, there are two kinds of content you can produce and publish on YouTube.

(usually asking people to subscribe to your channel).

If you're so inclined, producing and publishing a transcript of your YouTube video is also a sensible move.

- **Carefully Craft Your Title**

Your video titles should be short and snappy, offering a quick and intriguing insight into the content of your video. Don't forget to include your main keyword(s), too!

The best way to do this is to look at your title as if you'd never come across your brand before. Would you click on it? If you're not sure, change it. This often means moving any personal branding within the title to the end, so the main keywords appear first. It also means including episode numbers for serial content. And very importantly, be honest. Don't promise content that you don't deliver on.

- **Vary Your Content**

Speaking of content, in very broad terms, there are two kinds of content you can produce and publish on YouTube.

(usually asking people to subscribe to your channel).

If you're so inclined, producing and publishing a transcript of your YouTube video is also a sensible move.

- **Carefully Craft Your Title**

Your video titles should be short and snappy, offering a quick and intriguing insight into the content of your video. Don't forget to include your main keyword(s), too!

The best way to do this is to look at your title as if you'd never come across your brand before. Would you click on it? If you're not sure, change it. This often means moving any personal branding within the title to the end, so the main keywords appear first. It also means including episode numbers for serial content. And very importantly, be honest. Don't promise content that you don't deliver on.

- **Vary Your Content**

Speaking of content, in very broad terms, there are two kinds of content you can produce and publish on YouTube.

(usually asking people to subscribe to your channel).

If you're so inclined, producing and publishing a transcript of your YouTube video is also a sensible move.

- **Carefully Craft Your Title**

Your video titles should be short and snappy, offering a quick and intriguing insight into the content of your video. Don't forget to include your main keyword(s), too!

The best way to do this is to look at your title as if you'd never come across your brand before. Would you click on it? If you're not sure, change it. This often means moving any personal branding within the title to the end, so the main keywords appear first. It also means including episode numbers for serial content. And very importantly, be honest. Don't promise content that you don't deliver on.

- **Vary Your Content**

Speaking of content, in very broad terms, there are two kinds of content you can produce and publish on YouTube.

(usually asking people to subscribe to your channel).

If you're so inclined, producing and publishing a transcript of your YouTube video is also a sensible move.

- **Carefully Craft Your Title**

Your video titles should be short and snappy, offering a quick and intriguing insight into the content of your video. Don't forget to include your main keyword(s), too!

The best way to do this is to look at your title as if you'd never come across your brand before. Would you click on it? If you're not sure, change it. This often means moving any personal branding within the title to the end, so the main keywords appear first. It also means including episode numbers for serial content. And very importantly, be honest. Don't promise content that you don't deliver on.

- **Vary Your Content**

Speaking of content, in very broad terms, there are two kinds of content you can produce and publish on YouTube.

(usually asking people to subscribe to your channel).

If you're so inclined, producing and publishing a transcript of your YouTube video is also a sensible move.

- **Carefully Craft Your Title**

Your video titles should be short and snappy, offering a quick and intriguing insight into the content of your video. Don't forget to include your main keyword(s), too!

The best way to do this is to look at your title as if you'd never come across your brand before. Would you click on it? If you're not sure, change it. This often means moving any personal branding within the title to the end, so the main keywords appear first. It also means including episode numbers for serial content. And very importantly, be honest. Don't promise content that you don't deliver on.

- **Vary Your Content**

Speaking of content, in very broad terms, there are two kinds of content you can produce and publish on YouTube.

(usually asking people to subscribe to your channel).

If you're so inclined, producing and publishing a transcript of your YouTube video is also a sensible move.

- **Carefully Craft Your Title**

Your video titles should be short and snappy, offering a quick and intriguing insight into the content of your video. Don't forget to include your main keyword(s), too!

The best way to do this is to look at your title as if you'd never come across your brand before. Would you click on it? If you're not sure, change it. This often means moving any personal branding within the title to the end, so the main keywords appear first. It also means including episode numbers for serial content. And very importantly, be honest. Don't promise content that you don't deliver on.

- **Vary Your Content**

Speaking of content, in very broad terms, there are two kinds of content you can produce and publish on YouTube.

(usually asking people to subscribe to your channel).

If you're so inclined, producing and publishing a transcript of your YouTube video is also a sensible move.

- **Carefully Craft Your Title**

Your video titles should be short and snappy, offering a quick and intriguing insight into the content of your video. Don't forget to include your main keyword(s), too!

The best way to do this is to look at your title as if you'd never come across your brand before. Would you click on it? If you're not sure, change it. This often means moving any personal branding within the title to the end, so the main keywords appear first. It also means including episode numbers for serial content. And very importantly, be honest. Don't promise content that you don't deliver on.

- **Vary Your Content**

Speaking of content, in very broad terms, there are two kinds of content you can produce and publish on YouTube.

(usually asking people to subscribe to your channel).

If you're so inclined, producing and publishing a transcript of your YouTube video is also a sensible move.

- **Carefully Craft Your Title**

Your video titles should be short and snappy, offering a quick and intriguing insight into the content of your video. Don't forget to include your main keyword(s), too!

The best way to do this is to look at your title as if you'd never come across your brand before. Would you click on it? If you're not sure, change it. This often means moving any personal branding within the title to the end, so the main keywords appear first. It also means including episode numbers for serial content. And very importantly, be honest. Don't promise content that you don't deliver on.

- **Vary Your Content**

Speaking of content, in very broad terms, there are two kinds of content you can produce and publish on YouTube.

(usually asking people to subscribe to your channel).

If you're so inclined, producing and publishing a transcript of your YouTube video is also a sensible move.

- **Carefully Craft Your Title**

Your video titles should be short and snappy, offering a quick and intriguing insight into the content of your video. Don't forget to include your main keyword(s), too!

The best way to do this is to look at your title as if you'd never come across your brand before. Would you click on it? If you're not sure, change it. This often means moving any personal branding within the title to the end, so the main keywords appear first. It also means including episode numbers for serial content. And very importantly, be honest. Don't promise content that you don't deliver on.

- **Vary Your Content**

Speaking of content, in very broad terms, there are two kinds of content you can produce and publish on YouTube.

(usually asking people to subscribe to your channel).

If you're so inclined, producing and publishing a transcript of your YouTube video is also a sensible move.

- **Carefully Craft Your Title**

Your video titles should be short and snappy, offering a quick and intriguing insight into the content of your video. Don't forget to include your main keyword(s), too!

The best way to do this is to look at your title as if you'd never come across your brand before. Would you click on it? If you're not sure, change it. This often means moving any personal branding within the title to the end, so the main keywords appear first. It also means including episode numbers for serial content. And very importantly, be honest. Don't promise content that you don't deliver on.

- **Vary Your Content**

Speaking of content, in very broad terms, there are two kinds of content you can produce and publish on YouTube.

(usually asking people to subscribe to your channel).

If you're so inclined, producing and publishing a transcript of your YouTube video is also a sensible move.

- **Carefully Craft Your Title**

Your video titles should be short and snappy, offering a quick and intriguing insight into the content of your video. Don't forget to include your main keyword(s), too!

The best way to do this is to look at your title as if you'd never come across your brand before. Would you click on it? If you're not sure, change it. This often means moving any personal branding within the title to the end, so the main keywords appear first. It also means including episode numbers for serial content. And very importantly, be honest. Don't promise content that you don't deliver on.

- **Vary Your Content**

Speaking of content, in very broad terms, there are two kinds of content you can produce and publish on YouTube.

(usually asking people to subscribe to your channel).

If you're so inclined, producing and publishing a transcript of your YouTube video is also a sensible move.

- **Carefully Craft Your Title**

Your video titles should be short and snappy, offering a quick and intriguing insight into the content of your video. Don't forget to include your main keyword(s), too!

The best way to do this is to look at your title as if you'd never come across your brand before. Would you click on it? If you're not sure, change it. This often means moving any personal branding within the title to the end, so the main keywords appear first. It also means including episode numbers for serial content. And very importantly, be honest. Don't promise content that you don't deliver on.

- **Vary Your Content**

Speaking of content, in very broad terms, there are two kinds of content you can produce and publish on YouTube.

(usually asking people to subscribe to your channel).

If you're so inclined, producing and publishing a transcript of your YouTube video is also a sensible move.

- **Carefully Craft Your Title**

Your video titles should be short and snappy, offering a quick and intriguing insight into the content of your video. Don't forget to include your main keyword(s), too!

The best way to do this is to look at your title as if you'd never come across your brand before. Would you click on it? If you're not sure, change it. This often means moving any personal branding within the title to the end, so the main keywords appear first. It also means including episode numbers for serial content. And very importantly, be honest. Don't promise content that you don't deliver on.

- **Vary Your Content**

Speaking of content, in very broad terms, there are two kinds of content you can produce and publish on YouTube.

(usually asking people to subscribe to your channel).

If you're so inclined, producing and publishing a transcript of your YouTube video is also a sensible move.

- **Carefully Craft Your Title**

Your video titles should be short and snappy, offering a quick and intriguing insight into the content of your video. Don't forget to include your main keyword(s), too!

The best way to do this is to look at your title as if you'd never come across your brand before. Would you click on it? If you're not sure, change it. This often means moving any personal branding within the title to the end, so the main keywords appear first. It also means including episode numbers for serial content. And very importantly, be honest. Don't promise content that you don't deliver on.

- **Vary Your Content**

Speaking of content, in very broad terms, there are two kinds of content you can produce and publish on YouTube.

(usually asking people to subscribe to your channel).

If you're so inclined, producing and publishing a transcript of your YouTube video is also a sensible move.

- **Carefully Craft Your Title**

Your video titles should be short and snappy, offering a quick and intriguing insight into the content of your video. Don't forget to include your main keyword(s), too!

The best way to do this is to look at your title as if you'd never come across your brand before. Would you click on it? If you're not sure, change it. This often means moving any personal branding within the title to the end, so the main keywords appear first. It also means including episode numbers for serial content. And very importantly, be honest. Don't promise content that you don't deliver on.

- **Vary Your Content**

Speaking of content, in very broad terms, there are two kinds of content you can produce and publish on YouTube.

(usually asking people to subscribe to your channel).

If you're so inclined, producing and publishing a transcript of your YouTube video is also a sensible move.

- **Carefully Craft Your Title**

Your video titles should be short and snappy, offering a quick and intriguing insight into the content of your video. Don't forget to include your main keyword(s), too!

The best way to do this is to look at your title as if you'd never come across your brand before. Would you click on it? If you're not sure, change it. This often means moving any personal branding within the title to the end, so the main keywords appear first. It also means including episode numbers for serial content. And very importantly, be honest. Don't promise content that you don't deliver on.

- **Vary Your Content**

Speaking of content, in very broad terms, there are two kinds of content you can produce and publish on YouTube.

(usually asking people to subscribe to your channel).

If you're so inclined, producing and publishing a transcript of your YouTube video is also a sensible move.

- **Carefully Craft Your Title**

Your video titles should be short and snappy, offering a quick and intriguing insight into the content of your video. Don't forget to include your main keyword(s), too!

The best way to do this is to look at your title as if you'd never come across your brand before. Would you click on it? If you're not sure, change it. This often means moving any personal branding within the title to the end, so the main keywords appear first. It also means including episode numbers for serial content. And very importantly, be honest. Don't promise content that you don't deliver on.

- **Vary Your Content**

Speaking of content, in very broad terms, there are two kinds of content you can produce and publish on YouTube.

(usually asking people to subscribe to your channel).

If you're so inclined, producing and publishing a transcript of your YouTube video is also a sensible move.

- **Carefully Craft Your Title**

Your video titles should be short and snappy, offering a quick and intriguing insight into the content of your video. Don't forget to include your main keyword(s), too!

The best way to do this is to look at your title as if you'd never come across your brand before. Would you click on it? If you're not sure, change it. This often means moving any personal branding within the title to the end, so the main keywords appear first. It also means including episode numbers for serial content. And very importantly, be honest. Don't promise content that you don't deliver on.

- **Vary Your Content**

Speaking of content, in very broad terms, there are two kinds of content you can produce and publish on YouTube.

(usually asking people to subscribe to your channel).

If you're so inclined, producing and publishing a transcript of your YouTube video is also a sensible move.

- **Carefully Craft Your Title**

Your video titles should be short and snappy, offering a quick and intriguing insight into the content of your video. Don't forget to include your main keyword(s), too!

The best way to do this is to look at your title as if you'd never come across your brand before. Would you click on it? If you're not sure, change it. This often means moving any personal branding within the title to the end, so the main keywords appear first. It also means including episode numbers for serial content. And very importantly, be honest. Don't promise content that you don't deliver on.

- **Vary Your Content**

Speaking of content, in very broad terms, there are two kinds of content you can produce and publish on YouTube.

(usually asking people to subscribe to your channel).

If you're so inclined, producing and publishing a transcript of your YouTube video is also a sensible move.

- **Carefully Craft Your Title**

Your video titles should be short and snappy, offering a quick and intriguing insight into the content of your video. Don't forget to include your main keyword(s), too!

The best way to do this is to look at your title as if you'd never come across your brand before. Would you click on it? If you're not sure, change it. This often means moving any personal branding within the title to the end, so the main keywords appear first. It also means including episode numbers for serial content. And very importantly, be honest. Don't promise content that you don't deliver on.

- **Vary Your Content**

Speaking of content, in very broad terms, there are two kinds of content you can produce and publish on YouTube.

(usually asking people to subscribe to your channel).

If you're so inclined, producing and publishing a transcript of your YouTube video is also a sensible move.

- **Carefully Craft Your Title**

Your video titles should be short and snappy, offering a quick and intriguing insight into the content of your video. Don't forget to include your main keyword(s), too!

The best way to do this is to look at your title as if you'd never come across your brand before. Would you click on it? If you're not sure, change it. This often means moving any personal branding within the title to the end, so the main keywords appear first. It also means including episode numbers for serial content. And very importantly, be honest. Don't promise content that you don't deliver on.

- **Vary Your Content**

Speaking of content, in very broad terms, there are two kinds of content you can produce and publish on YouTube.

(usually asking people to subscribe to your channel).

If you're so inclined, producing and publishing a transcript of your YouTube video is also a sensible move.

- **Carefully Craft Your Title**

Your video titles should be short and snappy, offering a quick and intriguing insight into the content of your video. Don't forget to include your main keyword(s), too!

The best way to do this is to look at your title as if you'd never come across your brand before. Would you click on it? If you're not sure, change it. This often means moving any personal branding within the title to the end, so the main keywords appear first. It also means including episode numbers for serial content. And very importantly, be honest. Don't promise content that you don't deliver on.

- **Vary Your Content**

Speaking of content, in very broad terms, there are two kinds of content you can produce and publish on YouTube.

(usually asking people to subscribe to your channel).

If you're so inclined, producing and publishing a transcript of your YouTube video is also a sensible move.

- **Carefully Craft Your Title**

Your video titles should be short and snappy, offering a quick and intriguing insight into the content of your video. Don't forget to include your main keyword(s), too!

The best way to do this is to look at your title as if you'd never come across your brand before. Would you click on it? If you're not sure, change it. This often means moving any personal branding within the title to the end, so the main keywords appear first. It also means including episode numbers for serial content. And very importantly, be honest. Don't promise content that you don't deliver on.

- **Vary Your Content**

Speaking of content, in very broad terms, there are two kinds of content you can produce and publish on YouTube.

(usually asking people to subscribe to your channel).

If you're so inclined, producing and publishing a transcript of your YouTube video is also a sensible move.

- **Carefully Craft Your Title**

Your video titles should be short and snappy, offering a quick and intriguing insight into the content of your video. Don't forget to include your main keyword(s), too!

The best way to do this is to look at your title as if you'd never come across your brand before. Would you click on it? If you're not sure, change it. This often means moving any personal branding within the title to the end, so the main keywords appear first. It also means including episode numbers for serial content. And very importantly, be honest. Don't promise content that you don't deliver on.

- **Vary Your Content**

Speaking of content, in very broad terms, there are two kinds of content you can produce and publish on YouTube.

(usually asking people to subscribe to your channel).

If you're so inclined, producing and publishing a transcript of your YouTube video is also a sensible move.

- **Carefully Craft Your Title**

Your video titles should be short and snappy, offering a quick and intriguing insight into the content of your video. Don't forget to include your main keyword(s), too!

The best way to do this is to look at your title as if you'd never come across your brand before. Would you click on it? If you're not sure, change it. This often means moving any personal branding within the title to the end, so the main keywords appear first. It also means including episode numbers for serial content. And very importantly, be honest. Don't promise content that you don't deliver on.

- **Vary Your Content**

Speaking of content, in very broad terms, there are two kinds of content you can produce and publish on YouTube.

(usually asking people to subscribe to your channel).

If you're so inclined, producing and publishing a transcript of your YouTube video is also a sensible move.

- **Carefully Craft Your Title**

Your video titles should be short and snappy, offering a quick and intriguing insight into the content of your video. Don't forget to include your main keyword(s), too!

The best way to do this is to look at your title as if you'd never come across your brand before. Would you click on it? If you're not sure, change it. This often means moving any personal branding within the title to the end, so the main keywords appear first. It also means including episode numbers for serial content. And very importantly, be honest. Don't promise content that you don't deliver on.

- **Vary Your Content**

Speaking of content, in very broad terms, there are two kinds of content you can produce and publish on YouTube.

(usually asking people to subscribe to your channel).

If you're so inclined, producing and publishing a transcript of your YouTube video is also a sensible move.

- **Carefully Craft Your Title**

Your video titles should be short and snappy, offering a quick and intriguing insight into the content of your video. Don't forget to include your main keyword(s), too!

The best way to do this is to look at your title as if you'd never come across your brand before. Would you click on it? If you're not sure, change it. This often means moving any personal branding within the title to the end, so the main keywords appear first. It also means including episode numbers for serial content. And very importantly, be honest. Don't promise content that you don't deliver on.

- **Vary Your Content**

Speaking of content, in very broad terms, there are two kinds of content you can produce and publish on YouTube.

(usually asking people to subscribe to your channel).

If you're so inclined, producing and publishing a transcript of your YouTube video is also a sensible move.

- **Carefully Craft Your Title**

Your video titles should be short and snappy, offering a quick and intriguing insight into the content of your video. Don't forget to include your main keyword(s), too!

The best way to do this is to look at your title as if you'd never come across your brand before. Would you click on it? If you're not sure, change it. This often means moving any personal branding within the title to the end, so the main keywords appear first. It also means including episode numbers for serial content. And very importantly, be honest. Don't promise content that you don't deliver on.

- **Vary Your Content**

Speaking of content, in very broad terms, there are two kinds of content you can produce and publish on YouTube.

(usually asking people to subscribe to your channel).

If you're so inclined, producing and publishing a transcript of your YouTube video is also a sensible move.

- **Carefully Craft Your Title**

Your video titles should be short and snappy, offering a quick and intriguing insight into the content of your video. Don't forget to include your main keyword(s), too!

The best way to do this is to look at your title as if you'd never come across your brand before. Would you click on it? If you're not sure, change it. This often means moving any personal branding within the title to the end, so the main keywords appear first. It also means including episode numbers for serial content. And very importantly, be honest. Don't promise content that you don't deliver on.

- **Vary Your Content**

Speaking of content, in very broad terms, there are two kinds of content you can produce and publish on YouTube.

(usually asking people to subscribe to your channel).

If you're so inclined, producing and publishing a transcript of your YouTube video is also a sensible move.

- **Carefully Craft Your Title**

Your video titles should be short and snappy, offering a quick and intriguing insight into the content of your video. Don't forget to include your main keyword(s), too!

The best way to do this is to look at your title as if you'd never come across your brand before. Would you click on it? If you're not sure, change it. This often means moving any personal branding within the title to the end, so the main keywords appear first. It also means including episode numbers for serial content. And very importantly, be honest. Don't promise content that you don't deliver on.

- **Vary Your Content**

Speaking of content, in very broad terms, there are two kinds of content you can produce and publish on YouTube.

(usually asking people to subscribe to your channel).

If you're so inclined, producing and publishing a transcript of your YouTube video is also a sensible move.

- **Carefully Craft Your Title**

Your video titles should be short and snappy, offering a quick and intriguing insight into the content of your video. Don't forget to include your main keyword(s), too!

The best way to do this is to look at your title as if you'd never come across your brand before. Would you click on it? If you're not sure, change it. This often means moving any personal branding within the title to the end, so the main keywords appear first. It also means including episode numbers for serial content. And very importantly, be honest. Don't promise content that you don't deliver on.

- **Vary Your Content**

Speaking of content, in very broad terms, there are two kinds of content you can produce and publish on YouTube.

(usually asking people to subscribe to your channel).

If you're so inclined, producing and publishing a transcript of your YouTube video is also a sensible move.

- **Carefully Craft Your Title**

Your video titles should be short and snappy, offering a quick and intriguing insight into the content of your video. Don't forget to include your main keyword(s), too!

The best way to do this is to look at your title as if you'd never come across your brand before. Would you click on it? If you're not sure, change it. This often means moving any personal branding within the title to the end, so the main keywords appear first. It also means including episode numbers for serial content. And very importantly, be honest. Don't promise content that you don't deliver on.

- **Vary Your Content**

Speaking of content, in very broad terms, there are two kinds of content you can produce and publish on YouTube.

(usually asking people to subscribe to your channel).

If you're so inclined, producing and publishing a transcript of your YouTube video is also a sensible move.

- **Carefully Craft Your Title**

Your video titles should be short and snappy, offering a quick and intriguing insight into the content of your video. Don't forget to include your main keyword(s), too!

The best way to do this is to look at your title as if you'd never come across your brand before. Would you click on it? If you're not sure, change it. This often means moving any personal branding within the title to the end, so the main keywords appear first. It also means including episode numbers for serial content. And very importantly, be honest. Don't promise content that you don't deliver on.

- **Vary Your Content**

Speaking of content, in very broad terms, there are two kinds of content you can produce and publish on YouTube.

(usually asking people to subscribe to your channel).

If you're so inclined, producing and publishing a transcript of your YouTube video is also a sensible move.

- **Carefully Craft Your Title**

Your video titles should be short and snappy, offering a quick and intriguing insight into the content of your video. Don't forget to include your main keyword(s), too!

The best way to do this is to look at your title as if you'd never come across your brand before. Would you click on it? If you're not sure, change it. This often means moving any personal branding within the title to the end, so the main keywords appear first. It also means including episode numbers for serial content. And very importantly, be honest. Don't promise content that you don't deliver on.

- **Vary Your Content**

Speaking of content, in very broad terms, there are two kinds of content you can produce and publish on YouTube.

(usually asking people to subscribe to your channel).

If you're so inclined, producing and publishing a transcript of your YouTube video is also a sensible move.

- **Carefully Craft Your Title**

Your video titles should be short and snappy, offering a quick and intriguing insight into the content of your video. Don't forget to include your main keyword(s), too!

The best way to do this is to look at your title as if you'd never come across your brand before. Would you click on it? If you're not sure, change it. This often means moving any personal branding within the title to the end, so the main keywords appear first. It also means including episode numbers for serial content. And very importantly, be honest. Don't promise content that you don't deliver on.

- **Vary Your Content**

Speaking of content, in very broad terms, there are two kinds of content you can produce and publish on YouTube.

(usually asking people to subscribe to your channel).

If you're so inclined, producing and publishing a transcript of your YouTube video is also a sensible move.

- **Carefully Craft Your Title**

Your video titles should be short and snappy, offering a quick and intriguing insight into the content of your video. Don't forget to include your main keyword(s), too!

The best way to do this is to look at your title as if you'd never come across your brand before. Would you click on it? If you're not sure, change it. This often means moving any personal branding within the title to the end, so the main keywords appear first. It also means including episode numbers for serial content. And very importantly, be honest. Don't promise content that you don't deliver on.

- **Vary Your Content**

Speaking of content, in very broad terms, there are two kinds of content you can produce and publish on YouTube.

(usually asking people to subscribe to your channel).

If you're so inclined, producing and publishing a transcript of your YouTube video is also a sensible move.

- **Carefully Craft Your Title**

Your video titles should be short and snappy, offering a quick and intriguing insight into the content of your video. Don't forget to include your main keyword(s), too!

The best way to do this is to look at your title as if you'd never come across your brand before. Would you click on it? If you're not sure, change it. This often means moving any personal branding within the title to the end, so the main keywords appear first. It also means including episode numbers for serial content. And very importantly, be honest. Don't promise content that you don't deliver on.

- **Vary Your Content**

Speaking of content, in very broad terms, there are two kinds of content you can produce and publish on YouTube.

(usually asking people to subscribe to your channel).

If you're so inclined, producing and publishing a transcript of your YouTube video is also a sensible move.

- **Carefully Craft Your Title**

Your video titles should be short and snappy, offering a quick and intriguing insight into the content of your video. Don't forget to include your main keyword(s), too!

The best way to do this is to look at your title as if you'd never come across your brand before. Would you click on it? If you're not sure, change it. This often means moving any personal branding within the title to the end, so the main keywords appear first. It also means including episode numbers for serial content. And very importantly, be honest. Don't promise content that you don't deliver on.

- **Vary Your Content**

Speaking of content, in very broad terms, there are two kinds of content you can produce and publish on YouTube.

(usually asking people to subscribe to your channel).

If you're so inclined, producing and publishing a transcript of your YouTube video is also a sensible move.

- **Carefully Craft Your Title**

Your video titles should be short and snappy, offering a quick and intriguing insight into the content of your video. Don't forget to include your main keyword(s), too!

The best way to do this is to look at your title as if you'd never come across your brand before. Would you click on it? If you're not sure, change it. This often means moving any personal branding within the title to the end, so the main keywords appear first. It also means including episode numbers for serial content. And very importantly, be honest. Don't promise content that you don't deliver on.

- **Vary Your Content**

Speaking of content, in very broad terms, there are two kinds of content you can produce and publish on YouTube.

(usually asking people to subscribe to your channel).

If you're so inclined, producing and publishing a transcript of your YouTube video is also a sensible move.

- **Carefully Craft Your Title**

Your video titles should be short and snappy, offering a quick and intriguing insight into the content of your video. Don't forget to include your main keyword(s), too!

The best way to do this is to look at your title as if you'd never come across your brand before. Would you click on it? If you're not sure, change it. This often means moving any personal branding within the title to the end, so the main keywords appear first. It also means including episode numbers for serial content. And very importantly, be honest. Don't promise content that you don't deliver on.

- **Vary Your Content**

Speaking of content, in very broad terms, there are two kinds of content you can produce and publish on YouTube.

(usually asking people to subscribe to your channel).

If you're so inclined, producing and publishing a transcript of your YouTube video is also a sensible move.

- **Carefully Craft Your Title**

Your video titles should be short and snappy, offering a quick and intriguing insight into the content of your video. Don't forget to include your main keyword(s), too!

The best way to do this is to look at your title as if you'd never come across your brand before. Would you click on it? If you're not sure, change it. This often means moving any personal branding within the title to the end, so the main keywords appear first. It also means including episode numbers for serial content. And very importantly, be honest. Don't promise content that you don't deliver on.

- **Vary Your Content**

Speaking of content, in very broad terms, there are two kinds of content you can produce and publish on YouTube.

(usually asking people to subscribe to your channel).

If you're so inclined, producing and publishing a transcript of your YouTube video is also a sensible move.

- **Carefully Craft Your Title**

Your video titles should be short and snappy, offering a quick and intriguing insight into the content of your video. Don't forget to include your main keyword(s), too!

The best way to do this is to look at your title as if you'd never come across your brand before. Would you click on it? If you're not sure, change it. This often means moving any personal branding within the title to the end, so the main keywords appear first. It also means including episode numbers for serial content. And very importantly, be honest. Don't promise content that you don't deliver on.

- **Vary Your Content**

Speaking of content, in very broad terms, there are two kinds of content you can produce and publish on YouTube.

(usually asking people to subscribe to your channel).

If you're so inclined, producing and publishing a transcript of your YouTube video is also a sensible move.

- **Carefully Craft Your Title**

Your video titles should be short and snappy, offering a quick and intriguing insight into the content of your video. Don't forget to include your main keyword(s), too!

The best way to do this is to look at your title as if you'd never come across your brand before. Would you click on it? If you're not sure, change it. This often means moving any personal branding within the title to the end, so the main keywords appear first. It also means including episode numbers for serial content. And very importantly, be honest. Don't promise content that you don't deliver on.

- **Vary Your Content**

Speaking of content, in very broad terms, there are two kinds of content you can produce and publish on YouTube.

(usually asking people to subscribe to your channel).

If you're so inclined, producing and publishing a transcript of your YouTube video is also a sensible move.

- **Carefully Craft Your Title**

Your video titles should be short and snappy, offering a quick and intriguing insight into the content of your video. Don't forget to include your main keyword(s), too!

The best way to do this is to look at your title as if you'd never come across your brand before. Would you click on it? If you're not sure, change it. This often means moving any personal branding within the title to the end, so the main keywords appear first. It also means including episode numbers for serial content. And very importantly, be honest. Don't promise content that you don't deliver on.

- **Vary Your Content**

Speaking of content, in very broad terms, there are two kinds of content you can produce and publish on YouTube.

(usually asking people to subscribe to your channel).

If you're so inclined, producing and publishing a transcript of your YouTube video is also a sensible move.

- **Carefully Craft Your Title**

Your video titles should be short and snappy, offering a quick and intriguing insight into the content of your video. Don't forget to include your main keyword(s), too!

The best way to do this is to look at your title as if you'd never come across your brand before. Would you click on it? If you're not sure, change it. This often means moving any personal branding within the title to the end, so the main keywords appear first. It also means including episode numbers for serial content. And very importantly, be honest. Don't promise content that you don't deliver on.

- **Vary Your Content**

Speaking of content, in very broad terms, there are two kinds of content you can produce and publish on YouTube.

(usually asking people to subscribe to your channel).

If you're so inclined, producing and publishing a transcript of your YouTube video is also a sensible move.

- **Carefully Craft Your Title**

Your video titles should be short and snappy, offering a quick and intriguing insight into the content of your video. Don't forget to include your main keyword(s), too!

The best way to do this is to look at your title as if you'd never come across your brand before. Would you click on it? If you're not sure, change it. This often means moving any personal branding within the title to the end, so the main keywords appear first. It also means including episode numbers for serial content. And very importantly, be honest. Don't promise content that you don't deliver on.

- **Vary Your Content**

Speaking of content, in very broad terms, there are two kinds of content you can produce and publish on YouTube.

(usually asking people to subscribe to your channel).

If you're so inclined, producing and publishing a transcript of your YouTube video is also a sensible move.

- **Carefully Craft Your Title**

Your video titles should be short and snappy, offering a quick and intriguing insight into the content of your video. Don't forget to include your main keyword(s), too!

The best way to do this is to look at your title as if you'd never come across your brand before. Would you click on it? If you're not sure, change it. This often means moving any personal branding within the title to the end, so the main keywords appear first. It also means including episode numbers for serial content. And very importantly, be honest. Don't promise content that you don't deliver on.

- **Vary Your Content**

Speaking of content, in very broad terms, there are two kinds of content you can produce and publish on YouTube.

(usually asking people to subscribe to your channel).

If you're so inclined, producing and publishing a transcript of your YouTube video is also a sensible move.

- **Carefully Craft Your Title**

Your video titles should be short and snappy, offering a quick and intriguing insight into the content of your video. Don't forget to include your main keyword(s), too!

The best way to do this is to look at your title as if you'd never come across your brand before. Would you click on it? If you're not sure, change it. This often means moving any personal branding within the title to the end, so the main keywords appear first. It also means including episode numbers for serial content. And very importantly, be honest. Don't promise content that you don't deliver on.

- **Vary Your Content**

Speaking of content, in very broad terms, there are two kinds of content you can produce and publish on YouTube.

(usually asking people to subscribe to your channel).

If you're so inclined, producing and publishing a transcript of your YouTube video is also a sensible move.

- **Carefully Craft Your Title**

Your video titles should be short and snappy, offering a quick and intriguing insight into the content of your video. Don't forget to include your main keyword(s), too!

The best way to do this is to look at your title as if you'd never come across your brand before. Would you click on it? If you're not sure, change it. This often means moving any personal branding within the title to the end, so the main keywords appear first. It also means including episode numbers for serial content. And very importantly, be honest. Don't promise content that you don't deliver on.

- **Vary Your Content**

Speaking of content, in very broad terms, there are two kinds of content you can produce and publish on YouTube.

(usually asking people to subscribe to your channel).

If you're so inclined, producing and publishing a transcript of your YouTube video is also a sensible move.

- **Carefully Craft Your Title**

Your video titles should be short and snappy, offering a quick and intriguing insight into the content of your video. Don't forget to include your main keyword(s), too!

The best way to do this is to look at your title as if you'd never come across your brand before. Would you click on it? If you're not sure, change it. This often means moving any personal branding within the title to the end, so the main keywords appear first. It also means including episode numbers for serial content. And very importantly, be honest. Don't promise content that you don't deliver on.

- **Vary Your Content**

Speaking of content, in very broad terms, there are two kinds of content you can produce and publish on YouTube.

(usually asking people to subscribe to your channel).

If you're so inclined, producing and publishing a transcript of your YouTube video is also a sensible move.

- **Carefully Craft Your Title**

Your video titles should be short and snappy, offering a quick and intriguing insight into the content of your video. Don't forget to include your main keyword(s), too!

The best way to do this is to look at your title as if you'd never come across your brand before. Would you click on it? If you're not sure, change it. This often means moving any personal branding within the title to the end, so the main keywords appear first. It also means including episode numbers for serial content. And very importantly, be honest. Don't promise content that you don't deliver on.

- **Vary Your Content**

Speaking of content, in very broad terms, there are two kinds of content you can produce and publish on YouTube.

(usually asking people to subscribe to your channel).

If you're so inclined, producing and publishing a transcript of your YouTube video is also a sensible move.

- **Carefully Craft Your Title**

Your video titles should be short and snappy, offering a quick and intriguing insight into the content of your video. Don't forget to include your main keyword(s), too!

The best way to do this is to look at your title as if you'd never come across your brand before. Would you click on it? If you're not sure, change it. This often means moving any personal branding within the title to the end, so the main keywords appear first. It also means including episode numbers for serial content. And very importantly, be honest. Don't promise content that you don't deliver on.

- **Vary Your Content**

Speaking of content, in very broad terms, there are two kinds of content you can produce and publish on YouTube.

(usually asking people to subscribe to your channel).

If you're so inclined, producing and publishing a transcript of your YouTube video is also a sensible move.

- **Carefully Craft Your Title**

Your video titles should be short and snappy, offering a quick and intriguing insight into the content of your video. Don't forget to include your main keyword(s), too!

The best way to do this is to look at your title as if you'd never come across your brand before. Would you click on it? If you're not sure, change it. This often means moving any personal branding within the title to the end, so the main keywords appear first. It also means including episode numbers for serial content. And very importantly, be honest. Don't promise content that you don't deliver on.

- **Vary Your Content**

Speaking of content, in very broad terms, there are two kinds of content you can produce and publish on YouTube.

(usually asking people to subscribe to your channel).

If you're so inclined, producing and publishing a transcript of your YouTube video is also a sensible move.

- **Carefully Craft Your Title**

Your video titles should be short and snappy, offering a quick and intriguing insight into the content of your video. Don't forget to include your main keyword(s), too!

The best way to do this is to look at your title as if you'd never come across your brand before. Would you click on it? If you're not sure, change it. This often means moving any personal branding within the title to the end, so the main keywords appear first. It also means including episode numbers for serial content. And very importantly, be honest. Don't promise content that you don't deliver on.

- **Vary Your Content**

Speaking of content, in very broad terms, there are two kinds of content you can produce and publish on YouTube.

(usually asking people to subscribe to your channel).

If you're so inclined, producing and publishing a transcript of your YouTube video is also a sensible move.

- **Carefully Craft Your Title**

Your video titles should be short and snappy, offering a quick and intriguing insight into the content of your video. Don't forget to include your main keyword(s), too!

The best way to do this is to look at your title as if you'd never come across your brand before. Would you click on it? If you're not sure, change it. This often means moving any personal branding within the title to the end, so the main keywords appear first. It also means including episode numbers for serial content. And very importantly, be honest. Don't promise content that you don't deliver on.

- **Vary Your Content**

Speaking of content, in very broad terms, there are two kinds of content you can produce and publish on YouTube.

(usually asking people to subscribe to your channel).

If you're so inclined, producing and publishing a transcript of your YouTube video is also a sensible move.

- **Carefully Craft Your Title**

Your video titles should be short and snappy, offering a quick and intriguing insight into the content of your video. Don't forget to include your main keyword(s), too!

The best way to do this is to look at your title as if you'd never come across your brand before. Would you click on it? If you're not sure, change it. This often means moving any personal branding within the title to the end, so the main keywords appear first. It also means including episode numbers for serial content. And very importantly, be honest. Don't promise content that you don't deliver on.

- **Vary Your Content**

Speaking of content, in very broad terms, there are two kinds of content you can produce and publish on YouTube.

(usually asking people to subscribe to your channel).

If you're so inclined, producing and publishing a transcript of your YouTube video is also a sensible move.

- **Carefully Craft Your Title**

Your video titles should be short and snappy, offering a quick and intriguing insight into the content of your video. Don't forget to include your main keyword(s), too!

The best way to do this is to look at your title as if you'd never come across your brand before. Would you click on it? If you're not sure, change it. This often means moving any personal branding within the title to the end, so the main keywords appear first. It also means including episode numbers for serial content. And very importantly, be honest. Don't promise content that you don't deliver on.

- **Vary Your Content**

Speaking of content, in very broad terms, there are two kinds of content you can produce and publish on YouTube.

(usually asking people to subscribe to your channel).

If you're so inclined, producing and publishing a transcript of your YouTube video is also a sensible move.

- **Carefully Craft Your Title**

Your video titles should be short and snappy, offering a quick and intriguing insight into the content of your video. Don't forget to include your main keyword(s), too!

The best way to do this is to look at your title as if you'd never come across your brand before. Would you click on it? If you're not sure, change it. This often means moving any personal branding within the title to the end, so the main keywords appear first. It also means including episode numbers for serial content. And very importantly, be honest. Don't promise content that you don't deliver on.

- **Vary Your Content**

Speaking of content, in very broad terms, there are two kinds of content you can produce and publish on YouTube.

(usually asking people to subscribe to your channel).

If you're so inclined, producing and publishing a transcript of your YouTube video is also a sensible move.

- **Carefully Craft Your Title**

Your video titles should be short and snappy, offering a quick and intriguing insight into the content of your video. Don't forget to include your main keyword(s), too!

The best way to do this is to look at your title as if you'd never come across your brand before. Would you click on it? If you're not sure, change it. This often means moving any personal branding within the title to the end, so the main keywords appear first. It also means including episode numbers for serial content. And very importantly, be honest. Don't promise content that you don't deliver on.

- **Vary Your Content**

Speaking of content, in very broad terms, there are two kinds of content you can produce and publish on YouTube.

(usually asking people to subscribe to your channel).

If you're so inclined, producing and publishing a transcript of your YouTube video is also a sensible move.

- **Carefully Craft Your Title**

Your video titles should be short and snappy, offering a quick and intriguing insight into the content of your video. Don't forget to include your main keyword(s), too!

The best way to do this is to look at your title as if you'd never come across your brand before. Would you click on it? If you're not sure, change it. This often means moving any personal branding within the title to the end, so the main keywords appear first. It also means including episode numbers for serial content. And very importantly, be honest. Don't promise content that you don't deliver on.

- **Vary Your Content**

Speaking of content, in very broad terms, there are two kinds of content you can produce and publish on YouTube.

(usually asking people to subscribe to your channel).

If you're so inclined, producing and publishing a transcript of your YouTube video is also a sensible move.

- **Carefully Craft Your Title**

Your video titles should be short and snappy, offering a quick and intriguing insight into the content of your video. Don't forget to include your main keyword(s), too!

The best way to do this is to look at your title as if you'd never come across your brand before. Would you click on it? If you're not sure, change it. This often means moving any personal branding within the title to the end, so the main keywords appear first. It also means including episode numbers for serial content. And very importantly, be honest. Don't promise content that you don't deliver on.

- **Vary Your Content**

Speaking of content, in very broad terms, there are two kinds of content you can produce and publish on YouTube.

(usually asking people to subscribe to your channel).

If you're so inclined, producing and publishing a transcript of your YouTube video is also a sensible move.

- **Carefully Craft Your Title**

Your video titles should be short and snappy, offering a quick and intriguing insight into the content of your video. Don't forget to include your main keyword(s), too!

The best way to do this is to look at your title as if you'd never come across your brand before. Would you click on it? If you're not sure, change it. This often means moving any personal branding within the title to the end, so the main keywords appear first. It also means including episode numbers for serial content. And very importantly, be honest. Don't promise content that you don't deliver on.

- **Vary Your Content**

Speaking of content, in very broad terms, there are two kinds of content you can produce and publish on YouTube.

(usually asking people to subscribe to your channel).

If you're so inclined, producing and publishing a transcript of your YouTube video is also a sensible move.

- **Carefully Craft Your Title**

Your video titles should be short and snappy, offering a quick and intriguing insight into the content of your video. Don't forget to include your main keyword(s), too!

The best way to do this is to look at your title as if you'd never come across your brand before. Would you click on it? If you're not sure, change it. This often means moving any personal branding within the title to the end, so the main keywords appear first. It also means including episode numbers for serial content. And very importantly, be honest. Don't promise content that you don't deliver on.

- **Vary Your Content**

Speaking of content, in very broad terms, there are two kinds of content you can produce and publish on YouTube.

(usually asking people to subscribe to your channel).

If you're so inclined, producing and publishing a transcript of your YouTube video is also a sensible move.

- **Carefully Craft Your Title**

Your video titles should be short and snappy, offering a quick and intriguing insight into the content of your video. Don't forget to include your main keyword(s), too!

The best way to do this is to look at your title as if you'd never come across your brand before. Would you click on it? If you're not sure, change it. This often means moving any personal branding within the title to the end, so the main keywords appear first. It also means including episode numbers for serial content. And very importantly, be honest. Don't promise content that you don't deliver on.

- **Vary Your Content**

Speaking of content, in very broad terms, there are two kinds of content you can produce and publish on YouTube.

(usually asking people to subscribe to your channel).

If you're so inclined, producing and publishing a transcript of your YouTube video is also a sensible move.

- **Carefully Craft Your Title**

Your video titles should be short and snappy, offering a quick and intriguing insight into the content of your video. Don't forget to include your main keyword(s), too!

The best way to do this is to look at your title as if you'd never come across your brand before. Would you click on it? If you're not sure, change it. This often means moving any personal branding within the title to the end, so the main keywords appear first. It also means including episode numbers for serial content. And very importantly, be honest. Don't promise content that you don't deliver on.

- **Vary Your Content**

Speaking of content, in very broad terms, there are two kinds of content you can produce and publish on YouTube.

(usually asking people to subscribe to your channel).

If you're so inclined, producing and publishing a transcript of your YouTube video is also a sensible move.

- **Carefully Craft Your Title**

Your video titles should be short and snappy, offering a quick and intriguing insight into the content of your video. Don't forget to include your main keyword(s), too!

The best way to do this is to look at your title as if you'd never come across your brand before. Would you click on it? If you're not sure, change it. This often means moving any personal branding within the title to the end, so the main keywords appear first. It also means including episode numbers for serial content. And very importantly, be honest. Don't promise content that you don't deliver on.

- **Vary Your Content**

Speaking of content, in very broad terms, there are two kinds of content you can produce and publish on YouTube.

(usually asking people to subscribe to your channel).

If you're so inclined, producing and publishing a transcript of your YouTube video is also a sensible move.

- **Carefully Craft Your Title**

Your video titles should be short and snappy, offering a quick and intriguing insight into the content of your video. Don't forget to include your main keyword(s), too!

The best way to do this is to look at your title as if you'd never come across your brand before. Would you click on it? If you're not sure, change it. This often means moving any personal branding within the title to the end, so the main keywords appear first. It also means including episode numbers for serial content. And very importantly, be honest. Don't promise content that you don't deliver on.

- **Vary Your Content**

Speaking of content, in very broad terms, there are two kinds of content you can produce and publish on YouTube.

(usually asking people to subscribe to your channel).

If you're so inclined, producing and publishing a transcript of your YouTube video is also a sensible move.

- **Carefully Craft Your Title**

Your video titles should be short and snappy, offering a quick and intriguing insight into the content of your video. Don't forget to include your main keyword(s), too!

The best way to do this is to look at your title as if you'd never come across your brand before. Would you click on it? If you're not sure, change it. This often means moving any personal branding within the title to the end, so the main keywords appear first. It also means including episode numbers for serial content. And very importantly, be honest. Don't promise content that you don't deliver on.

- **Vary Your Content**

Speaking of content, in very broad terms, there are two kinds of content you can produce and publish on YouTube.

(usually asking people to subscribe to your channel).

If you're so inclined, producing and publishing a transcript of your YouTube video is also a sensible move.

- **Carefully Craft Your Title**

Your video titles should be short and snappy, offering a quick and intriguing insight into the content of your video. Don't forget to include your main keyword(s), too!

The best way to do this is to look at your title as if you'd never come across your brand before. Would you click on it? If you're not sure, change it. This often means moving any personal branding within the title to the end, so the main keywords appear first. It also means including episode numbers for serial content. And very importantly, be honest. Don't promise content that you don't deliver on.

- **Vary Your Content**

Speaking of content, in very broad terms, there are two kinds of content you can produce and publish on YouTube.

(usually asking people to subscribe to your channel).

If you're so inclined, producing and publishing a transcript of your YouTube video is also a sensible move.

- **Carefully Craft Your Title**

Your video titles should be short and snappy, offering a quick and intriguing insight into the content of your video. Don't forget to include your main keyword(s), too!

The best way to do this is to look at your title as if you'd never come across your brand before. Would you click on it? If you're not sure, change it. This often means moving any personal branding within the title to the end, so the main keywords appear first. It also means including episode numbers for serial content. And very importantly, be honest. Don't promise content that you don't deliver on.

- **Vary Your Content**

Speaking of content, in very broad terms, there are two kinds of content you can produce and publish on YouTube.

(usually asking people to subscribe to your channel).

If you're so inclined, producing and publishing a transcript of your YouTube video is also a sensible move.

- **Carefully Craft Your Title**

Your video titles should be short and snappy, offering a quick and intriguing insight into the content of your video. Don't forget to include your main keyword(s), too!

The best way to do this is to look at your title as if you'd never come across your brand before. Would you click on it? If you're not sure, change it. This often means moving any personal branding within the title to the end, so the main keywords appear first. It also means including episode numbers for serial content. And very importantly, be honest. Don't promise content that you don't deliver on.

- **Vary Your Content**

Speaking of content, in very broad terms, there are two kinds of content you can produce and publish on YouTube.

(usually asking people to subscribe to your channel).

If you're so inclined, producing and publishing a transcript of your YouTube video is also a sensible move.

- **Carefully Craft Your Title**

Your video titles should be short and snappy, offering a quick and intriguing insight into the content of your video. Don't forget to include your main keyword(s), too!

The best way to do this is to look at your title as if you'd never come across your brand before. Would you click on it? If you're not sure, change it. This often means moving any personal branding within the title to the end, so the main keywords appear first. It also means including episode numbers for serial content. And very importantly, be honest. Don't promise content that you don't deliver on.

- **Vary Your Content**

Speaking of content, in very broad terms, there are two kinds of content you can produce and publish on YouTube.

(usually asking people to subscribe to your channel).

If you're so inclined, producing and publishing a transcript of your YouTube video is also a sensible move.

- **Carefully Craft Your Title**

Your video titles should be short and snappy, offering a quick and intriguing insight into the content of your video. Don't forget to include your main keyword(s), too!

The best way to do this is to look at your title as if you'd never come across your brand before. Would you click on it? If you're not sure, change it. This often means moving any personal branding within the title to the end, so the main keywords appear first. It also means including episode numbers for serial content. And very importantly, be honest. Don't promise content that you don't deliver on.

- **Vary Your Content**

Speaking of content, in very broad terms, there are two kinds of content you can produce and publish on YouTube.

(usually asking people to subscribe to your channel).

If you're so inclined, producing and publishing a transcript of your YouTube video is also a sensible move.

- **Carefully Craft Your Title**

Your video titles should be short and snappy, offering a quick and intriguing insight into the content of your video. Don't forget to include your main keyword(s), too!

The best way to do this is to look at your title as if you'd never come across your brand before. Would you click on it? If you're not sure, change it. This often means moving any personal branding within the title to the end, so the main keywords appear first. It also means including episode numbers for serial content. And very importantly, be honest. Don't promise content that you don't deliver on.

- **Vary Your Content**

Speaking of content, in very broad terms, there are two kinds of content you can produce and publish on YouTube.

(usually asking people to subscribe to your channel).

If you're so inclined, producing and publishing a transcript of your YouTube video is also a sensible move.

- **Carefully Craft Your Title**

Your video titles should be short and snappy, offering a quick and intriguing insight into the content of your video. Don't forget to include your main keyword(s), too!

The best way to do this is to look at your title as if you'd never come across your brand before. Would you click on it? If you're not sure, change it. This often means moving any personal branding within the title to the end, so the main keywords appear first. It also means including episode numbers for serial content. And very importantly, be honest. Don't promise content that you don't deliver on.

- **Vary Your Content**

Speaking of content, in very broad terms, there are two kinds of content you can produce and publish on YouTube.

(usually asking people to subscribe to your channel).

If you're so inclined, producing and publishing a transcript of your YouTube video is also a sensible move.

- **Carefully Craft Your Title**

Your video titles should be short and snappy, offering a quick and intriguing insight into the content of your video. Don't forget to include your main keyword(s), too!

The best way to do this is to look at your title as if you'd never come across your brand before. Would you click on it? If you're not sure, change it. This often means moving any personal branding within the title to the end, so the main keywords appear first. It also means including episode numbers for serial content. And very importantly, be honest. Don't promise content that you don't deliver on.

- **Vary Your Content**

Speaking of content, in very broad terms, there are two kinds of content you can produce and publish on YouTube.

(usually asking people to subscribe to your channel).

If you're so inclined, producing and publishing a transcript of your YouTube video is also a sensible move.

- **Carefully Craft Your Title**

Your video titles should be short and snappy, offering a quick and intriguing insight into the content of your video. Don't forget to include your main keyword(s), too!

The best way to do this is to look at your title as if you'd never come across your brand before. Would you click on it? If you're not sure, change it. This often means moving any personal branding within the title to the end, so the main keywords appear first. It also means including episode numbers for serial content. And very importantly, be honest. Don't promise content that you don't deliver on.

- **Vary Your Content**

Speaking of content, in very broad terms, there are two kinds of content you can produce and publish on YouTube.

(usually asking people to subscribe to your channel).

If you're so inclined, producing and publishing a transcript of your YouTube video is also a sensible move.

- **Carefully Craft Your Title**

Your video titles should be short and snappy, offering a quick and intriguing insight into the content of your video. Don't forget to include your main keyword(s), too!

The best way to do this is to look at your title as if you'd never come across your brand before. Would you click on it? If you're not sure, change it. This often means moving any personal branding within the title to the end, so the main keywords appear first. It also means including episode numbers for serial content. And very importantly, be honest. Don't promise content that you don't deliver on.

- **Vary Your Content**

Speaking of content, in very broad terms, there are two kinds of content you can produce and publish on YouTube.

(usually asking people to subscribe to your channel).

If you're so inclined, producing and publishing a transcript of your YouTube video is also a sensible move.

- **Carefully Craft Your Title**

Your video titles should be short and snappy, offering a quick and intriguing insight into the content of your video. Don't forget to include your main keyword(s), too!

The best way to do this is to look at your title as if you'd never come across your brand before. Would you click on it? If you're not sure, change it. This often means moving any personal branding within the title to the end, so the main keywords appear first. It also means including episode numbers for serial content. And very importantly, be honest. Don't promise content that you don't deliver on.

- **Vary Your Content**

Speaking of content, in very broad terms, there are two kinds of content you can produce and publish on YouTube.

(usually asking people to subscribe to your channel).

If you're so inclined, producing and publishing a transcript of your YouTube video is also a sensible move.

- **Carefully Craft Your Title**

Your video titles should be short and snappy, offering a quick and intriguing insight into the content of your video. Don't forget to include your main keyword(s), too!

The best way to do this is to look at your title as if you'd never come across your brand before. Would you click on it? If you're not sure, change it. This often means moving any personal branding within the title to the end, so the main keywords appear first. It also means including episode numbers for serial content. And very importantly, be honest. Don't promise content that you don't deliver on.

- **Vary Your Content**

Speaking of content, in very broad terms, there are two kinds of content you can produce and publish on YouTube.

(usually asking people to subscribe to your channel).

If you're so inclined, producing and publishing a transcript of your YouTube video is also a sensible move.

- **Carefully Craft Your Title**

Your video titles should be short and snappy, offering a quick and intriguing insight into the content of your video. Don't forget to include your main keyword(s), too!

The best way to do this is to look at your title as if you'd never come across your brand before. Would you click on it? If you're not sure, change it. This often means moving any personal branding within the title to the end, so the main keywords appear first. It also means including episode numbers for serial content. And very importantly, be honest. Don't promise content that you don't deliver on.

- **Vary Your Content**

Speaking of content, in very broad terms, there are two kinds of content you can produce and publish on YouTube.

(usually asking people to subscribe to your channel).

If you're so inclined, producing and publishing a transcript of your YouTube video is also a sensible move.

- **Carefully Craft Your Title**

Your video titles should be short and snappy, offering a quick and intriguing insight into the content of your video. Don't forget to include your main keyword(s), too!

The best way to do this is to look at your title as if you'd never come across your brand before. Would you click on it? If you're not sure, change it. This often means moving any personal branding within the title to the end, so the main keywords appear first. It also means including episode numbers for serial content. And very importantly, be honest. Don't promise content that you don't deliver on.

- **Vary Your Content**

Speaking of content, in very broad terms, there are two kinds of content you can produce and publish on YouTube.

(usually asking people to subscribe to your channel).

If you're so inclined, producing and publishing a transcript of your YouTube video is also a sensible move.

- **Carefully Craft Your Title**

Your video titles should be short and snappy, offering a quick and intriguing insight into the content of your video. Don't forget to include your main keyword(s), too!

The best way to do this is to look at your title as if you'd never come across your brand before. Would you click on it? If you're not sure, change it. This often means moving any personal branding within the title to the end, so the main keywords appear first. It also means including episode numbers for serial content. And very importantly, be honest. Don't promise content that you don't deliver on.

- **Vary Your Content**

Speaking of content, in very broad terms, there are two kinds of content you can produce and publish on YouTube.

(usually asking people to subscribe to your channel).

If you're so inclined, producing and publishing a transcript of your YouTube video is also a sensible move.

- **Carefully Craft Your Title**

Your video titles should be short and snappy, offering a quick and intriguing insight into the content of your video. Don't forget to include your main keyword(s), too!

The best way to do this is to look at your title as if you'd never come across your brand before. Would you click on it? If you're not sure, change it. This often means moving any personal branding within the title to the end, so the main keywords appear first. It also means including episode numbers for serial content. And very importantly, be honest. Don't promise content that you don't deliver on.

- **Vary Your Content**

Speaking of content, in very broad terms, there are two kinds of content you can produce and publish on YouTube.

(usually asking people to subscribe to your channel).

If you're so inclined, producing and publishing a transcript of your YouTube video is also a sensible move.

- **Carefully Craft Your Title**

Your video titles should be short and snappy, offering a quick and intriguing insight into the content of your video. Don't forget to include your main keyword(s), too!

The best way to do this is to look at your title as if you'd never come across your brand before. Would you click on it? If you're not sure, change it. This often means moving any personal branding within the title to the end, so the main keywords appear first. It also means including episode numbers for serial content. And very importantly, be honest. Don't promise content that you don't deliver on.

- **Vary Your Content**

Speaking of content, in very broad terms, there are two kinds of content you can produce and publish on YouTube.

(usually asking people to subscribe to your channel).

If you're so inclined, producing and publishing a transcript of your YouTube video is also a sensible move.

- **Carefully Craft Your Title**

Your video titles should be short and snappy, offering a quick and intriguing insight into the content of your video. Don't forget to include your main keyword(s), too!

The best way to do this is to look at your title as if you'd never come across your brand before. Would you click on it? If you're not sure, change it. This often means moving any personal branding within the title to the end, so the main keywords appear first. It also means including episode numbers for serial content. And very importantly, be honest. Don't promise content that you don't deliver on.

- **Vary Your Content**

Speaking of content, in very broad terms, there are two kinds of content you can produce and publish on YouTube.

(usually asking people to subscribe to your channel).

If you're so inclined, producing and publishing a transcript of your YouTube video is also a sensible move.

- **Carefully Craft Your Title**

Your video titles should be short and snappy, offering a quick and intriguing insight into the content of your video. Don't forget to include your main keyword(s), too!

The best way to do this is to look at your title as if you'd never come across your brand before. Would you click on it? If you're not sure, change it. This often means moving any personal branding within the title to the end, so the main keywords appear first. It also means including episode numbers for serial content. And very importantly, be honest. Don't promise content that you don't deliver on.

- **Vary Your Content**

Speaking of content, in very broad terms, there are two kinds of content you can produce and publish on YouTube.

(usually asking people to subscribe to your channel).

If you're so inclined, producing and publishing a transcript of your YouTube video is also a sensible move.

- **Carefully Craft Your Title**

Your video titles should be short and snappy, offering a quick and intriguing insight into the content of your video. Don't forget to include your main keyword(s), too!

The best way to do this is to look at your title as if you'd never come across your brand before. Would you click on it? If you're not sure, change it. This often means moving any personal branding within the title to the end, so the main keywords appear first. It also means including episode numbers for serial content. And very importantly, be honest. Don't promise content that you don't deliver on.

- **Vary Your Content**

Speaking of content, in very broad terms, there are two kinds of content you can produce and publish on YouTube.

(usually asking people to subscribe to your channel).

If you're so inclined, producing and publishing a transcript of your YouTube video is also a sensible move.

- **Carefully Craft Your Title**

Your video titles should be short and snappy, offering a quick and intriguing insight into the content of your video. Don't forget to include your main keyword(s), too!

The best way to do this is to look at your title as if you'd never come across your brand before. Would you click on it? If you're not sure, change it. This often means moving any personal branding within the title to the end, so the main keywords appear first. It also means including episode numbers for serial content. And very importantly, be honest. Don't promise content that you don't deliver on.

- **Vary Your Content**

Speaking of content, in very broad terms, there are two kinds of content you can produce and publish on YouTube.

(usually asking people to subscribe to your channel).

If you're so inclined, producing and publishing a transcript of your YouTube video is also a sensible move.

- **Carefully Craft Your Title**

Your video titles should be short and snappy, offering a quick and intriguing insight into the content of your video. Don't forget to include your main keyword(s), too!

The best way to do this is to look at your title as if you'd never come across your brand before. Would you click on it? If you're not sure, change it. This often means moving any personal branding within the title to the end, so the main keywords appear first. It also means including episode numbers for serial content. And very importantly, be honest. Don't promise content that you don't deliver on.

- **Vary Your Content**

Speaking of content, in very broad terms, there are two kinds of content you can produce and publish on YouTube.

(usually asking people to subscribe to your channel).

If you're so inclined, producing and publishing a transcript of your YouTube video is also a sensible move.

- **Carefully Craft Your Title**

Your video titles should be short and snappy, offering a quick and intriguing insight into the content of your video. Don't forget to include your main keyword(s), too!

The best way to do this is to look at your title as if you'd never come across your brand before. Would you click on it? If you're not sure, change it. This often means moving any personal branding within the title to the end, so the main keywords appear first. It also means including episode numbers for serial content. And very importantly, be honest. Don't promise content that you don't deliver on.

- **Vary Your Content**

Speaking of content, in very broad terms, there are two kinds of content you can produce and publish on YouTube.

(usually asking people to subscribe to your channel).

If you're so inclined, producing and publishing a transcript of your YouTube video is also a sensible move.

- **Carefully Craft Your Title**

Your video titles should be short and snappy, offering a quick and intriguing insight into the content of your video. Don't forget to include your main keyword(s), too!

The best way to do this is to look at your title as if you'd never come across your brand before. Would you click on it? If you're not sure, change it. This often means moving any personal branding within the title to the end, so the main keywords appear first. It also means including episode numbers for serial content. And very importantly, be honest. Don't promise content that you don't deliver on.

- **Vary Your Content**

Speaking of content, in very broad terms, there are two kinds of content you can produce and publish on YouTube.

(usually asking people to subscribe to your channel).

If you're so inclined, producing and publishing a transcript of your YouTube video is also a sensible move.

- **Carefully Craft Your Title**

Your video titles should be short and snappy, offering a quick and intriguing insight into the content of your video. Don't forget to include your main keyword(s), too!

The best way to do this is to look at your title as if you'd never come across your brand before. Would you click on it? If you're not sure, change it. This often means moving any personal branding within the title to the end, so the main keywords appear first. It also means including episode numbers for serial content. And very importantly, be honest. Don't promise content that you don't deliver on.

- **Vary Your Content**

Speaking of content, in very broad terms, there are two kinds of content you can produce and publish on YouTube.

(usually asking people to subscribe to your channel).

If you're so inclined, producing and publishing a transcript of your YouTube video is also a sensible move.

- **Carefully Craft Your Title**

Your video titles should be short and snappy, offering a quick and intriguing insight into the content of your video. Don't forget to include your main keyword(s), too!

The best way to do this is to look at your title as if you'd never come across your brand before. Would you click on it? If you're not sure, change it. This often means moving any personal branding within the title to the end, so the main keywords appear first. It also means including episode numbers for serial content. And very importantly, be honest. Don't promise content that you don't deliver on.

- **Vary Your Content**

Speaking of content, in very broad terms, there are two kinds of content you can produce and publish on YouTube.

(usually asking people to subscribe to your channel).

If you're so inclined, producing and publishing a transcript of your YouTube video is also a sensible move.

- **Carefully Craft Your Title**

Your video titles should be short and snappy, offering a quick and intriguing insight into the content of your video. Don't forget to include your main keyword(s), too!

The best way to do this is to look at your title as if you'd never come across your brand before. Would you click on it? If you're not sure, change it. This often means moving any personal branding within the title to the end, so the main keywords appear first. It also means including episode numbers for serial content. And very importantly, be honest. Don't promise content that you don't deliver on.

- **Vary Your Content**

Speaking of content, in very broad terms, there are two kinds of content you can produce and publish on YouTube.

(usually asking people to subscribe to your channel).

If you're so inclined, producing and publishing a transcript of your YouTube video is also a sensible move.

- **Carefully Craft Your Title**

Your video titles should be short and snappy, offering a quick and intriguing insight into the content of your video. Don't forget to include your main keyword(s), too!

The best way to do this is to look at your title as if you'd never come across your brand before. Would you click on it? If you're not sure, change it. This often means moving any personal branding within the title to the end, so the main keywords appear first. It also means including episode numbers for serial content. And very importantly, be honest. Don't promise content that you don't deliver on.

- **Vary Your Content**

Speaking of content, in very broad terms, there are two kinds of content you can produce and publish on YouTube.

(usually asking people to subscribe to your channel).

If you're so inclined, producing and publishing a transcript of your YouTube video is also a sensible move.

- **Carefully Craft Your Title**

Your video titles should be short and snappy, offering a quick and intriguing insight into the content of your video. Don't forget to include your main keyword(s), too!

The best way to do this is to look at your title as if you'd never come across your brand before. Would you click on it? If you're not sure, change it. This often means moving any personal branding within the title to the end, so the main keywords appear first. It also means including episode numbers for serial content. And very importantly, be honest. Don't promise content that you don't deliver on.

- **Vary Your Content**

Speaking of content, in very broad terms, there are two kinds of content you can produce and publish on YouTube.

(usually asking people to subscribe to your channel).

If you're so inclined, producing and publishing a transcript of your YouTube video is also a sensible move.

- **Carefully Craft Your Title**

Your video titles should be short and snappy, offering a quick and intriguing insight into the content of your video. Don't forget to include your main keyword(s), too!

The best way to do this is to look at your title as if you'd never come across your brand before. Would you click on it? If you're not sure, change it. This often means moving any personal branding within the title to the end, so the main keywords appear first. It also means including episode numbers for serial content. And very importantly, be honest. Don't promise content that you don't deliver on.

- **Vary Your Content**

Speaking of content, in very broad terms, there are two kinds of content you can produce and publish on YouTube.

(usually asking people to subscribe to your channel).

If you're so inclined, producing and publishing a transcript of your YouTube video is also a sensible move.

- **Carefully Craft Your Title**

Your video titles should be short and snappy, offering a quick and intriguing insight into the content of your video. Don't forget to include your main keyword(s), too!

The best way to do this is to look at your title as if you'd never come across your brand before. Would you click on it? If you're not sure, change it. This often means moving any personal branding within the title to the end, so the main keywords appear first. It also means including episode numbers for serial content. And very importantly, be honest. Don't promise content that you don't deliver on.

- **Vary Your Content**

Speaking of content, in very broad terms, there are two kinds of content you can produce and publish on YouTube.

(usually asking people to subscribe to your channel).

If you're so inclined, producing and publishing a transcript of your YouTube video is also a sensible move.

- **Carefully Craft Your Title**

Your video titles should be short and snappy, offering a quick and intriguing insight into the content of your video. Don't forget to include your main keyword(s), too!

The best way to do this is to look at your title as if you'd never come across your brand before. Would you click on it? If you're not sure, change it. This often means moving any personal branding within the title to the end, so the main keywords appear first. It also means including episode numbers for serial content. And very importantly, be honest. Don't promise content that you don't deliver on.

- **Vary Your Content**

Speaking of content, in very broad terms, there are two kinds of content you can produce and publish on YouTube.